Women in Ministry

Women in Ministry

QUESTIONS AND ANSWERS
IN THE EXPLORATION OF A CALLING

Shannon Nicole Smythe

FOREWORD BY
Robert W. Wall

CASCADE *Books* • Eugene, Oregon

WOMEN IN MINISTRY
Questions and Answers in the Exploration of a Calling

Copyright © 2015 Shannon Nicole Smythe. All rights reserved. Except for brief quotations in critical publications or reviews, no part of this book may be reproduced in any manner without prior written permission from the publisher. Write: Permissions, Wipf and Stock Publishers, 199 W. 8th Ave., Suite 3, Eugene, OR 97401.

Cascade Books
An Imprint of Wipf and Stock Publishers
199 W. 8th Ave., Suite 3
Eugene, OR 97401

www.wipfandstock.com

ISBN 13: 978-1-62564-512-8

Cataloging-in-Publication data:

Smythe, Shannon Nicole

    Women in ministry : questions and answers in the exploration of a calling / Shannon Nicole Smythe

    xviii + 96 p. ; 21.5 cm. —Includes bibliographical references.

    ISBN 13: 978-1-62564-512-8

    1. Women clergy. 2. Ordination of women. I. Title.

BV676 S79 2015

Manufactured in the U.S.A.

Dedicated to the students, past, present, and future,
of Seattle Pacific University

Contents

Foreword

In a pair of provocative and controversial books, Ephraim Radner calls the church catholic to repentance for the divisive practices that have dismembered the body of Christ throughout its sometimes tragic history.[1] He laments, for instance, the church's liberal tendency to tolerate its own divisions as though doing so engages in a ministry of reconciliation. In his trenchant narrative of the church's history, Radner plots a wide variety of historical moments when God's people have actively inflicted wounds upon each other by maintaining their "walls of enmity" along theological and ideological lines. Drawing upon the biblical typology of a divided Israel, he claims God has withdrawn the holy Spirit from a divided church because its presence there has been compromised by members who see one another as enemies and fail to love one another. God's Spirit has no reason dwelling in a hostile place where divisions between Christians have replaced the loving practices of God's salvation-creating grace.

The problem Radner addresses in his second book is more practical but still hard-hitting. He observes the problem facing today's church is not that Christians are unaware of the differences that divide them or even that their destructive behaviors and incriminating words towards each other dishonor their risen Lord. Christians get this, Radner claims, but only in the abstract. The real problem is that they tend to view these debilitating divisions, typically around difficult hot-button issues, as merely routine in a social world characterized by fiercely waged culture wars. Radner

---

1. Radner, *The End of the Church; A Brutal Unity.*

ix

sees that the new truth of a fallen creation is a divided church, one that lives as if the sin that divides us has greater capital than the grace that unites us. The shameful result, he concludes, is a benign neglect of a fractured church, resulting in an even more intractable disunity and rendering its gospel claims of Christ's self-denying love unconvincing to non-believers.

Now to the purpose of this book. In many Christian congregations and college classrooms, debates over the ordination and ministry of women continue in just this same vein, creating hurtful and debilitating divisions among believers. This new book, written by Dr. Shannon Smythe, leans into those inhospitable places to invite serious readers into a process of discernment that intends to lead them, and women especially, into a fresh awareness of their sacred calling to a ministry of the gospel. The sequence of her carefully ordered chapters, moving between theology and Scripture, church history and testimony, guides a process that can change minds and inspire new directions on this topic. Dr. Smythe is well aware that both kinds of decisions are often responses of costly obedience, as it was for her; but that precisely for this reason, inviting readers into this process of learning can transform the ethos of both classroom and congregation into a more hospitable home for the empowering work of the triune God.

She has constructed a fitting context for the Spirit's ministry of reconciliation, not so much by preaching to readers or even by providing hard evidence that demands a particular verdict, but by inviting them to participate in the communal practice of studying Scripture together in dialogue with the church's theological traditions and the testimonies of faithful women—women whose experiences of life with God and a call to Christian ministry provide for us all good examples of obedience to God's word. Apropos of a "companion" like this one, she finally asks readers, at the end of their learning curve, to reflect in deeply personal ways upon the truth they have found in their study of Scripture, theology, and history, confirmed by the testimony of others, which then enables the Spirit to direct (or redirect) them forward in the ways of God. This amen is not so much an altar call but the endgame of a process of holy discernment that prompts a free choice, an obedient decision that lines the disciple up with the mind of Christ.

Dr. Smythe places at the epicenter of this discernment process a carefully directed dialogue between Scripture and theology. A theological interpretation of Scripture does not bring a particular modern "criticism" to the biblical text but, rather, a range of theological interests as ancient as the church. Strong students not only recognize that Scripture bears authoritative witness to God's saving work in history, they expect that a faithful reading of Scripture targets the loving relationship between God and God's people. That is, if Scripture is approached as a revelatory text, then any Spirit-directed application by its faithful readers should result in a more mature understanding of God's word whose effective yield is a more satisfying life with God.

The practical problem of such a task, of course, is the abundant surplus, not scarcity, of theological resources at the church's disposal in its Scriptures. In fact, one could say that the Bible, from beginning to end, is about the relationship between God and God's people: what does it truly mean to be God's people and do as they ought? In part, this is because the Bible is the church's holy Scripture, shaped and sized from beginning to end in the company of the holy Spirit to size and shape a holy church that is also one, catholic, and apostolic. Toward this end, every Scripture is God-breathed to inform, form, and reform God's people into a covenant-keeping community, a light to the nations.

There remains a practical problem of how best to organize inspired yet diverse biblical texts into a working resource for faithful readers to use with theological profit. Dr. Smythe offers readers a careful selection of sacred texts because she has a bone to pick; that is, the dialogue between selected biblical passages and her core belief in the triune God guides her to where theological goods are mined that most likely will help her readers engage in their process of discernment. But they are also selected with a full awareness that a primary reason why people disagree over this topic concerns how to read the very passages she has selected to study. While the reasons for these disagreements are complex, often involving social worlds as much as linguistic analysis, the practices for doing so are properly communal. This is a book that encourages interested people to read, study, and discuss Scripture *together*. Worshiping God and studying Scripture *together* cultivates those characteristics that enable earnest Christians to resist the tendency of allowing disagreements between them to harden into non-negotiable positions that occasion harsh and hurtful accusations of others on the other side of the divide. This provides a context for both understanding and reconciliation.

This book is deeply grounded in the church's confession that its Scripture—every bit of it—is God's inspired and inspiring word. Any attentive engagement with what Scripture says, especially if it demands our repentance, as I think this book does, not only recognizes the holiness of the biblical texts that are studied—even those well-known "texts of terror" such as 1 Timothy 2:9–15—but their proper reading and application within the economy of grace. That is, Scripture is the sanctified auxiliary of the holy Spirit who teaches us God's word and draws us into loving communion with God and with all our neighbors. The practice of studying biblical passages together commends the belief that Scripture's authority cannot subsist apart from an engaged *community* of readers who carefully and prayerfully wait upon the Spirit to disclose God's truth to them.

The welcome addition of short vignettes of the saints recalled from the church's past and testimonies of faithful women currently engaged in ministry, which are scattered throughout the book, underscore the belief that the best guides to a right interpretation of Scripture are those whose core beliefs and lives conform to God's way of salvation and so to the subject matter of Scripture. Testimony is a crucial practice of the Wesleyan communion to which I belong. This is because we believe that God's saving grace is directly and tangibly experienced. Grace is not a theological abstraction, then, something that goes undetected in public and is known only by the intellect and then communicated to others by "God-talk." More than debates of theological positions, firsthand stories of an experienced grace are often a compelling source for understanding the real meaning of Scripture. They create a wonderful dialogue; Scripture and testimonies of an experienced grace are not only personally illuminating, the act of sharing it with others grants it a certain theological authority with the effect of convincing people of the gospel's truth.

I am deeply thankful for this book, which I consider a gift to the church, and for Dr. Smythe's willingness to tackle this topic with evident passion and confident grace. May God bless its use to help bring understanding and healing.

Robert W. Wall
The Paul T. Walls Professor of Scripture and Wesleyan Studies
Seattle Pacific University

Acknowledgments

This book is the result of Rob Wall's insistence that our previous version, *Women With a Passion for Ministry: A Catechism*, published by Seattle Pacific University in 2004 for the campus, should be revised and expanded for a wider audience. I am grateful to him for his support and belief in this project, and for the shared enthusiasm of Chris Spinks at Cascade Books. I have a very fond memory of a working lunch on a beautiful sunny day on the Seattle waterfront with Rob, along with Priscilla Pope-Levison and Celeste Cranston, both ordained ministers and faculty and staff, respectively, at Seattle Pacific University, in which we hatched a plan for turning the little catechism, which had been in wide use by small groups and classes around campus, into something more.

This project was born originally out of many conversations and experiences during my time as an undergraduate student (1998–2002) at SPU when I was in the process of sorting out my own thoughts about the topic of women in ministry, coming as I did from a conservative church and family who did not support the full participation of women in all aspects of ministry. It reflects the many things I learned about the relation between Scripture, theology, church history, and faithful Christian discipleship while taking classes from the faculty of the School of Theology at SPU, including Kerry Dearborn, Bob Drovdahl, Jack Levison, Dave Nienhuis, Priscilla Pope-Levison, Frank Spina, Rick Steele, and Rob Wall. The revised and expanded book is also reflective of my time at Princeton Theological Seminary, where I took a whole cadre of courses with an emphasis in women's studies during my Master of Divinity program, served for two years as the co-moderator of the Women's Center, became friends and classmates with count-less women called and gifted to ordained ministry, and eventually concentrated in systematic theology for my PhD program. Finally, my experiences from my time of ministry in three different Pres-byterian Church (USA) congregations, including mentorship by the Reverends Joyce MacKichan Walker and Nancy Mikoski, and ruling elder Carol Wehrheim, have profoundly shaped the final form of the project in ways seen and unseen.

As I worked on revisions to the original project, I had the blessing of productive conversations and helpful written feedback from three women—Kim Castelo, Christy Mesaros-Winckles, and Kelsey Rorem, who each gave me wise and on-target suggestions for questions and topics either to add, revise, or expand on. In addition, I am grateful to the women in my writing group, Janel Erchinger-Davis and Nancy Pagh, who kept me accountable to my writing goals and celebrated with me with wine and cake when I met them. Finally, this updated book is all the stronger for the inclusion of the personal testimonies of Susan Sytsma Bratt, Erin Hayes, Jennifer Herold, Julie Hoplamazian, Cari Pattison, and Traci Smith. I am deeply honored for their willingness to share their stories of calling to ministry so openly in this book. Every time I read their stories, I am encouraged and inspired.

My constant companion and unrelenting cheerleader in life and ministry is my husband, Kevin Subers. Without his unwaver-ing commitment and love, this book would not have seen the light of day. And for keeping me grounded in the every day reality of sand, dirt, tractors, squirrels, and more, I have my toddler son, Micah, and dog, Linus, to thank.

Introduction

A GUIDE TO USING THIS BOOK

The questions and answers that form the core structure of this book attempt to set forth not only a key set of topics commonly raised in discussions surrounding the issue of women in ministry but also to provide, for those open to the explorative journey, an affirmative approach to the full inclusion of women in all forms and roles of ministry in the church. The question-answer format, similar to the catechetical method of teaching used through the history of the Christian church, has the benefit of allowing the questions to shape the information presented. The questions and answers are by no means exhaustive, but they intend to be a well-rounded approach to the topic. While there are many specific studies available on the question of women in ministry, this book intends to approach the issue from a broad perspective, covering issues related to Scripture, theology, tradition, and experience—the four sources believers have always consulted when seeking to discern the mind of God. That being said, there are many other resources that delve into the various themes and issues explored in this book in much more detail than what we can do here. Interested readers would do well to consult the bibliography for sources with more detailed accounts of the various issues. In addition to the question-answer format, each chapter includes Bible Study and Discussion Questions as well as Reflection Questions that are designed to allow readers to interact with the material, reflect, and make their own discoveries through biblical study. These questions are ideal for use by small groups, in classroom discussions, or for personal study.

A final word about a rather unique element to the book is in order. Peppered throughout the book are two things: (1) a collection of twelve brief biographical sketches of women in the history of the church who have been used dynamically by God in their work and ministry, and (2) six testimonies by currently ordained ministers (and one who is in the ordination process) re-counting their own calling, struggles, and perspectives as women. The intended effect is one in which the reader would find not only parallels between women in ministry throughout church history and women in ministry today but also that the reader would be compelled towards greater thoughtfulness and hope by relating specific names and stories to a topic too-often removed from its concrete bearings in the lives of specific individuals and church communities. If I have learned one thing from my own explora-tions and journey with this topic, it is that hearts are changed and minds opened by the opportunity to hear from, interact with, and be exposed to women who have been, are, and will be called, gifted, and used mightily in church ministry. This final element, then, is my way of providing that opportunity to the readers through the pages of the book.

1

A Brief Overview of Women in Ministry

WHAT IS THE ISSUE?

Here it is. Does Scripture restrict the scope and nature of women's participation in Christian ministry on the basis of gender? This question, while sometimes stated in other ways throughout the history of the church, is the crux of the issue. The question is not new. Yet its ongoing relevance cannot be overstated, and the negative answers given to it profoundly shape not only church communities but countless lives of women and men, from the young girl who grows up without seeing any women ministers, to the church community whose view of God, not to mention its pastoral and missional ministries, are all made smaller by limiting the leadership to only 50 percent of the community. These are the concerns of those, like myself, who take a strong position in favor of the full participation of gifted and qualified women in all forms of Christian ministry, and especially in ordained roles. Therefore, while recognizing the diversity of views on the issue by Christian denominations and various congregations and not wanting to bend the rules of right interpretation or Christian discernment in my favor, the position championed in this book is this: when a faithful follower of Jesus considers the church's entire "canonical heritage" (i.e., the rule of faith, Scripture, theology, church history, biographies of exemplary Christians, and real-life experiences of

God's people), it seems clear that God indeed calls women to lead and minister to church congregations as well as to serve in other, higher, denomination-specific offices and roles.

What Is at Stake?

Without a doubt, the discussion of women in ministry has divided many well-meaning Christians throughout history, making this an issue that can further isolate and polarize those in the church who disagree on the topic and arrive at differing conclusions. This study strives to be an open and safe context for readers to wrestle with the issues at hand. It is all right to be upset and disagree with what is put forth in this book. At the same time, *thoughtful* objections and *reasonable* responses are needed if Christians are to resist misunderstandings that lead to unhelpful quarreling and unnecessary escalation. It is only in the context of an open and truthful environment that the church can move forward on this issue. Such an environment will never look like total agreement or harmony, but it will instead reflect a more accurate and respectful understanding of the positions held by those on each side while honoring the faithfulness of each side to the Lord of the church, never trying to call into question the legitimate status of the Christian believer or community.

That being said, there is no doubt that the church is hindered when any of its members are prevented from using their Spirit-given gifts to build up the body of Christ and participate with God's ministry of reconciliation in the world. Nineteenth-century Methodist holiness evangelist Phoebe Palmer once critiqued the church by remarking that it has buried women's gifts in a Potter's Field.[1] Many gifted women are eager to obey God's call on their lives but have been convinced by other believers that to follow through on their call to ministry is, in fact, not God's will for them.

---

1. The Potter's Field refers to land outside of Jerusalem used for the burial of strangers and foreigners. The field is referenced in Matt 27:1–10. Jewish leaders used the thirty coins Judas returned to them after he betrayed Jesus to purchase a potter's field to bury strangers and foreigners.

What they are being denied is the opportunity to share fully in God's mission in the world as members of the apostolic community. For this apostolic mission, Scripture is clear that the laborers are few, while the harvest is great (Matt 9:37). God's people must work collaboratively, contributing their unique gifts to the service of God, with the hope that all people might be saved. God has prepared good works in advance for men and women (Eph 2:10). The church is called to empower all members towards those good works (Heb 10:24–25).

Bible Study and Discussion Questions

Read Matt 9:35–38

1. What does Jesus do in all the cities and villages?
2. Why does Jesus have compassion on the crowd?
3. In your own words, what is the job of the laborers?
4. Why do you think there are so few laborers today?

Read Eph 2:10

1. What is the relationship between believers and God?
2. What is the significance of being "created in Christ Jesus"?

For Reflection

1. Why is the issue of women in ministry today a topic that often stirs us so deeply?
2. Consider the following potential fears some might have around the issue of women in ministry. Some might fear not being true to Scripture. Others might worry that women are too emotional. Still others, perhaps, may be concerned/fearful because the topic is so new to them and they have never really seen women

in leadership before. Reflect on your own thoughts about these fears or others you might have or can think of.

Perpetua, martyred c. 203

Saint Perpetua, born as a noblewoman in the third century, had access to education. She was also a catechumen of the church and thus had the benefit of receiving training in the Christian faith. She is the author of the earliest extant extra-biblical material written by a Christian woman. At about the age of twenty-one, she was arrested because of her Christian faith. Like many other martyrs of her day, she was held in prison in the Coliseum and eventually fed to lions while a crowd looked on. At that time, women were considered equal in martyrdom. Through history, the church has looked on the story of Perpetua as an example of a faithful follower of Jesus who remained strong in the face of persecution and trials.

Testimony: The Reverend Erin Hayes

The Reverend Erin Hayes grew up in the rolling hills of Port Murray, New Jersey. She has degrees from Albright College and Princeton Theological Seminary. When not busy serving as the pastor of First Presbyterian Church of Rahway, New Jersey, you will find her reading a great book, running, or in search of the best, local coffee shop.

At the age of thirteen, I led worship in my tiny Baptist church. Maybe the congregation knew where I would end up. All I knew was that I loved being with God. When it came time to go to college and declare my major, I felt an unexplainable stirring inside of me. In every way, I hungered to know God. One night, driving home from a prayer meeting, I heard a voice say, "I want you to be a minister." My response of "yes," led to a bachelor's degree in religious studies followed by a master of divinity degree.

After seminary, I felt another stirring and restlessness in my heart. I knew deep down that God was knocking on the door of my heart to invite me to become an ordained pastor. Like a toddler

4

in the midst of a tantrum, I dropped my weight and complained I was not worthy. What I did not realize was that it was not about how equipped I was at the time, but about my willingness to say yes to God again. God wanted to do a great work in me. And that work has been hard and rewarding all at the same time. While serving a church and finishing my ordination requirements for my denomination, I had many "come to Jesus" prayer meetings in my apartment.

As a young, bi-racial woman I believe that my call has been a series of reconciliations between myself and the world. As part of the ordination process in my denomination, candidates are taken "under care" of a presbytery. In my presbytery, I was the only woman of color during all five years of my time "under care." In fact, the day I came before the committee to share with them my sense of call to ordained ministry, one of the members said, "Why would you, a person of color, want to come here?" To this day I hear that question as an assault, "Do you think you are worthy of joining us?"

Throughout the years, I have watched the look of surprise come over people's faces when I introduce myself as a pastor. Once, another female pastor, even, challenged my education and calling from the pulpit. Recently, I led a funeral with two hundred and fifty people in attendance. After the service, a woman came and told me, "You looked like a twelve year old up there." Nevermind my eleven years in ministry or that we are the same age.

I get weary thinking I have to prove myself. Like Hagar, roaming through the wilderness, making a new path, I stop to breathe and remember that God called me. I hear the voice of my paternal great-grandmother cheer me on from heaven. I believe that the Holy One invited me to share all that I am with the world. It is true; your average pastor does not wear kinky twists and a nose ring or claim both Hungarian and African-American heritage. I am not average. I never will be. But I serve a God who is not preoccupied with average—a God who makes the impossible possible. For me, this is not only my source of hope but also my place of renewal.

For Reflection

Consider and reflect on the dual dynamic of race and gender that is at play in the call story above. Where is the challenge, and where is the hope in the story?

2

Theology & Women in Ministry

WHY IS THE CHURCH'S RULE OF FAITH IMPORTANT?

The "rule of faith" summarizes the heart of Christian faith and serves as a theological boundary marker for Christian thought and living.[1] In other words, the "rule of faith" is separate from Scripture yet informed by it.[2] The core beliefs of faith provide criteria for evaluating various interpretations of Scripture.[3] The "rule of faith" is grounded in belief in the triune God and relates the essential beliefs of Christianity together by God's self-revelation in Christ and our experience of God's presence throughout history. The basic content of our beliefs is what Jesus Christ said and did, as well as the entire narrative of salvation history, beginning with creation and ending with the final consummation. These two elements form the rule's core. Yet the rule of faith is not static. Rather, it tells of God's dynamic work in the world and, for that reason, is an able guide by which the issue of women in ministry may be discerned.

1. Wall, "Reading the Bible from within Our Traditions," 89.

2. "The Rule of Faith thus resides in a reciprocal relationship with Scripture, with the former constraining what can properly be designated as 'Christian' readings of the biblical texts and the latter reminding Christians of the heterogeneity of those narrative and confessional formulations that reside not only in Scripture but often also within the 'rules.'" Ibid., 106.

3. Ibid., 89.

WHY IS THEOLOGY IMPORTANT FOR THIS ISSUE?

While it could be argued that the issue of women in ministry is not the core of the central Christian beliefs or church doctrine, the issue is nevertheless important and related to the theological doctrines that are central to Christian faith. If, at its simplest, the task of theology is to provide a way for the church to reflect on its understanding of God, humanity, the world, and all of the inter-relationships and themes contained therein, then the connection between theology and the issue of women in ministry becomes apparent.

The issue of women in ministry can be classified under the thematic umbrella of male/female relations. In terms of theology and doctrine, such topics belong to the realm of theological an-thropology, the theological study of what it means to be human and to be in relationship with one another. Theological anthro-pology, as a subfield of theological study, is closely related to and impacted by the theological themes explored in the doctrine of God, not to mention Christology and pneumatology. For instance, how we understand the being and character of God impacts our way of thinking about what it means to be human and to be in relationship with God and one another. One common line of thinking about the issue of women in ministry, then, considers the relationship of how we understand the triune God—God's way of relating and being as a Trinity—and what that might mean for how we understand ways of human relating one to another as male and female. Another theological connection comes in relationship to Christology and the issue of women in ministry. How does our understanding of the person and work of Jesus Christ impact the way we think about what it means to be human and to be in rela-tionship with one another? Finally, how does our understanding of the Holy Spirit contribute to the stance we take on the issue? And so, all of the sudden, we notice that the particular question of women in ministry is closely connected to key theological themes and doctrines of the Christian faith.

How Does Our Understanding of the Trinity Relate to Gender Relations?[4]

This is a very important question to ask. Theologians who articulate a doctrine of the Trinity called social Trinitarianism[5] often appeal to their understanding of the Trinity as a basis for an egalitarian view of gender roles. However, those who advocate a complementarian view of gender roles also find a basis in this social doctrine of the Trinity. Of course their argument works a little differently than the egalitarian argument from the social Trinity. The fact that both sides appeal to the social Trinity might lead one to want to throw up her hands in defeat, but more can be said to clarify matters.

While it is important to explore the relationship of the doctrine of the Trinity to gender roles, we get into tricky waters when we want to relate gender relations to the social Trinity. A core affirmation of social Trinitarianism is the claim that Father, Son, and Spirit are united as a communion of distinct persons. By contrast, the traditional articulation of the doctrine of the Trinity upholds that the unity of the three "hypostases," or divine persons, is located in the one divine nature or substance. Social Trinitarianism, however, says that Father, Son, and Spirit are three independent centers of consciousness, each with their own distinct intellect and will, which are nevertheless united as a perichoretic communion.

---

4. I am indebted to David W. Congdon for his clarity of thought on this very question, which helped me solidify my own thinking on this topic. See Congdon, "Trinity, Gender, and Subordination."

5. It is important to note that there are many different versions of social Trinitarianism but all of them share a focus on using social analogies in defining and describing the Trinity so as to draw correlations to human society. Social Trinitarianism defines the three persons of the triune God in terms of relationality. In other words, the three persons are united as a perichoretic communion of distinct persons with independent centers of consciousness, including their own distinct intellects, wills, and energies of operations. Social Trinitarianism locates the unity of the triune God in the idea of perichoresis rather than in the traditional idea of unity in terms of one divine nature or substance.

This social understanding of the Trinity, however, really only works if our definition of the three persons of the Trinity is defined by the modern psychological notion of "person," which is entirely different from the original meaning of the word "person" (*hypostasis*) as it was traditionally used to describe the Trinity. The ancient meaning of "person" (*hypostasis*) was based on the idea of an individual essence, or a particular mode of one nature or substance. Yet with the modern concept of "person," the attribute of self-consciousness is introduced into the doctrine of the Trinity. This leads to a distortion of the doctrine of the Trinity. Instead of one God in three modalities of the same substance, as the traditional doctrine intended, the social Trinity has three distinct self-conscious agents. For all practical purposes this is the same as saying that there are three deities instead of one God. The result, in other words, of using the modern concept of "person" to describe the three modalities within the Godhead is that not even the concept of perichoresis, which social Trinitarianism makes a lot out of, can unite God into a single agent. Here's why. The doctrine of perichoresis refers to the mysterious interpenetration of each divine "person" (*hypostasis*) into the other two, such that no separation or division of agency is possible. In essence, perichoresis supports the Trinitarian rule put in place by Augustine to guard against tritheism, which states that the external acts of the Trinity are indivisible. In social Trinitarianism, perichoresis is about a unity of the wills of the three persons. This results in the triune persons sounding more like three individual human persons acting in harmony on an agreed upon task. In contrast to this, the divine unity among the triune persons of God comes from an identity of the same will not from a fellowship of three different wills. What this demonstrates is that the danger of social Trinitarianism in conversations about gender relations is the projection of human ideals upon God.

Another important element in need of clarification in discussions about the relationship of gender equality and the Trinity is the biblical concept of male and female "in the image of God" (*imago Dei*). Notably, in the history of Christianity, theologians have never agreed on the meaning of *imago Dei*. At some point, however, there was a change in the type of questions being asked about the *imago Dei*. Instead of asking "How do we image God?" theologians began to ask "what makes human beings different from the animals?" This new question arose from an underlying assumption that the image of God was something humans possessed intrinsically rather than something we enact. Thus, the idea of the *imago Dei* as an inherent feature of our humanity has often meant that people assume being men and women "in the image of God" has a particular gendered relationality that is somehow similar to the relationality we find in the Trinity. The problem with assuming that men and women have intrinsic ways of relating to each other that is based on the Trinity not only leads to theological nonsense it also nullifies the theological concept that the image of God in us could be lost through sin and restored only through our reconciliation to God in Christ.

Again, as we saw with social Trinitarianism and gender relations, no logical analogy can be drawn from the unique relationality in the Trinity to humanity unless we first start with what human ideals of relationality between men and women should look like and project that back onto God. The fundamental problem with this kind of an analogy between Trinitarian relations and human relations is its failure to take into consideration the wholly otherness of God. God is absolutely transcendent and totally other than the world and humanity. This means that there is no analogy to human gender in God because God is wholly beyond human attributes like sexual differentiation. Church tradition has always affirmed this. Gregory of Nyssa writes, "The divine is neither male nor female (for how could such a thing be contemplated in divinity?)."[6]

So, can we say anything positive about our understanding of the Trinity in connection to gender relations? A better way to see the connection between the triune God and humanity is on the level of an analogy of faith (*analogia fidei*). Under this line of thinking, humanity is analogous to God only on the basis of faith.

6. Gregory, *Song of Songs*, 145; quoted in Tanner, *Christ the Key*, 212.

The *imago Dei* is not a human quality inherent to human nature, it is only a gift that comes to us by grace. It is only through faith that humanity comes to receive the *imago Dei* as the Spirit conforms us to Christ. Instead of the *imago Dei* looking differently in us depending on whether we are male or female, it is wholly inclusive of both genders. Male and female alike are called to become participants in the mission of God through the saving work of Christ and the empowerment of the Spirit. Insofar as we participate in the mission of the triune God in the world, both genders image God equally.

How Does God's Revelation in Jesus Give Us a Picture of Male and Female Relationships?

As indicated in the answer to the previous question, it is only by way of God's revelation in Jesus Christ that we can even begin to speak rightly about our human relationships. Jesus reveals to us what reconciliation looks like on all levels: with God, with one another, and with creation. It is the event of the incarnation that opens up an avenue for understanding how both genders image God. With Jesus' incarnation, we discover that what is important is not his particular gender, but the saving significance of his full humanity for all people. In other words, in the incarnation we see that the triune God, in the human person of Jesus, stood in the place of all sinners, male and female alike, living a life of perfect obedience to the will of the Father and suffering death on the cross for us and in our place. It is this mission of the triune God into the world in Christ, by the power of the Spirit, to affect our reconciliation, that establishes the ground for our likeness to God. Theologian Kathryn Tanner gives a helpful explanation:

> [T]he trinity itself enters our world in Christ to show us
> how human relations are to be reformed in its image.
> . . . The trinity in the economy does not close the gap
> by making Trinitarian relations something like human
> ones, but by actually incorporating the human into its
> very own life through the incarnation. We are therefore

not called to imitate the trinity by way of the incarnation but brought to participate in it. . . . In Christ we are therefore shown what the trinity looks like when it includes the human, and what humanity looks like when it is taken up within the trinity's own relationships. . . . The gap between divine and human is not closed here by making the two similar to one another, but by joining the two very different things—humanity and divinity, which remain very different things—into one in Christ via the incarnation. Trinitarian relations need not be like human relations in order for humans to be taken up into them. . . . The trinity is not brought down to our level as a model for us to imitate; our hope is that we might be raised up to its level.[7]

What Tanner highlights is Jesus' revelation of what it means to be human in the incarnation shows us all humanity is called into relationship with the Trinity through the one person, Jesus Christ. This is not the same thing as saying humanity is called into the same relationship with one another as that of the Father, Son, and Spirit. "The trinity does not therefore in any obvious way establish the internal structure of human community, the unity of the trinity being what makes human society one, the diversity of the persons establishing its internal complexity."[8] Therefore, it is the mission of "the one divine Son and the one divine Spirit . . . [to] make human society one; we are one, as the Pauline texts suggest, because we all have the same Spirit and because we are all members of the one Son."[9]

But, we can say a bit more about our relations with one another when we consider Jesus' own relationship with other people. Looking at the life of Jesus, we find he "relates to other people in highly unusual ways,"[10] which is a reflection of his relations to the Father and the Spirit. "A life empowered by the Spirit in service to the mission of the Father for the world means that Jesus is with

7. Tanner, *Christ the Key*, 234–36.

8. Ibid., 238.

9. Ibid.

10. Ibid., 240.

and for us, and that we, in turn, are to be with and for one another, in the way that mission specifies. The character of that mission, as Jesus' own way of life makes clear, is to inaugurate a life-brimming, Spirit-filled community of human beings akin to Jesus in their relations with God."[11] All of us, men and women alike, are to be with and for one another in such a way that we are contributing to the flourishing of the Spirit-filled community of Jesus followers. What we can see by this is that there is no place for prioritizing one gender over another nor is there any room for hierarchical distinctions. We are all related equally to the Trinity through the person of Jesus. And our co-humanity as male and female is equally represented and equally drawn into the life of Jesus.

When we bear in mind that just as Jesus is with and for us so are we to be with and for one another, then we can also see that certain, temporarily assumed roles among us as servant leaders and as those who mutually submit to one another also has an appropriate place in our male and female relations. Mutual submission, however, "is not permanent and does not imply a hierarchy; rather, it is flexible, dynamic, and based on self-giving love."[12] Mutual submission is based, in other words, on the mission of Jesus. So, too, is servant leadership. The point of servant leadership is for "those in power to use that gift to empower others, especially those who are weak."[13] "This taking up of a temporary role at a specific time and within a specific community is just one concrete way in which we believers fulfill the command of Christ to love one another. The greatest command of all, of course, is to love the Lord our God. The active giving of oneself is connected to this greatest of all commandments."[14] When we disconnect male and female relations from distorted ideas such as hierarchy, complementarity, and any other attempt to generalize and make static and permanent any particular gender's role and characteristics, we are freed up to thoughtfully consider individual gifting, contextual dynamics, and

11. Ibid.
12. Padgett, *As Christ Submits to the Church*, 127.
13. Ibid.
14. Ibid., 127–28.

14

other community or culture-specific realities. Not only does this allow for a more Spirit-filled approach (which we will discuss in more depth below), it also keeps clear that our overall aim in life is to grow in our love of and service to both God and neighbor.

How Are We to Understand the Gifts of the Holy Spirit in Relationship to Men and Women?

The dramatic beginning of the church, in the event of Pentecost and fulfillment of Joel's prophecy (Acts 2:1–36), demonstrates clearly that the gifting of the Spirit has pushed out beyond all former barriers of race, gender, economic, and social status. There simply are no longer any standard divisions among people when it comes to the Spirit's outpouring. The work of the Spirit among the people of God is to equip each of us for our unique roles in the kingdom work of God on earth. "The powers-that-be explode at Pentecost, in which the spirit is poured out on all flesh, and no less richly on female slaves than on powerful men."[15] Godly men and women are given the gifts of prophecy, teaching, serving, encouraging, contributing to the needs of others, leading, and showing mercy (Rom 12:6–8). Gifts are given according to God's grace not gender, sex, or any other "worldly" classification. The sending of the Spirit and gifting of God's people are signs of hope to a broken world that new creation life has already been inaugurated in the death and resurrection of Christ. The kingdom of God turns the paradigms of the world upside down.

As the church is called to be a radically, inclusive, new Christian community, one specific way it witnesses to the in-breaking of God's kingdom in the world is by operating out of a "gift-based" ministry framework. Such a framework allows the church to operate first and foremost out of the Spirit's gifting of individuals rather than out of "old order" roles and structures, which are passing away. It also acknowledges something often forgotten. The New Testament does not speak much, if at all, about the nature and

---

15. Levison, "Thrill Ride: Acts 1–2."

structure of church offices. Concerns over whether women as well as men are allowed to lead in specific church positions is a concern from a later time in the church than what we find recorded in the letters of the New Testament. Paul, in particular, simply does not take up the question. "The New Testament evidence is that the Holy Spirit is gender inclusive, gifting both men and women, and thus potentially setting the whole body free for all the many parts to minister and in various ways to give leadership to the others."[16] Prioritizing the gifting of the Spirit over gender is not only more faithful to the emphasis within Scripture; it also frees us up to focus on ministry specifics rather than questions of authority. The important questions of if and how all of God's people are being ministered to and are using their gifts for ministry are allowed to take center stage.

Bible Study and Discussion Questions

1. In your own words, describe your understanding of the proper analogical relationship of the Trinity to men and women.
2. How do you understand the role and gifting of the Spirit in relationship to men and women called to ministry?

Read Gen 3:14–19 and Rom 6:6–11, 14

1. What are the effects of the curse?
2. Having died with Christ, how are we to understand the effects of the curse?

Read Rom 12:4–8

1. According to these verses, who is Paul addressing?
2. What is the basis of the different gifts?

16. Fee, "The Priority of Spirit Gifting," 254.

3. Why do we need all of the gifts given to the church?

For Reflection

What should be the starting point in understanding what the Bible says about women in ministry?

Julian of Norwich: 1342–ca 1416

The English mystic, Julian, was an anchorite for the city of Norwich. An anchorite is one who lives in solitude by withdrawing to a cell to pray for the community. Her goal was to be completely focused on Christ, our anchor in heaven. She prayed to know the mind of Christ and to experience the pain and suffering he experienced on the cross. In a series of experiential visions, she received sixteen "showings," or revelations, of the love of God. Julian recorded these revelations from God, which were about creation and fall, the crucifixion of Christ, grace, and prayer. Her writings are the first of any English woman. Mystic and theologian, Julian's spirituality has contributed much to the church's understanding of the motherly nature of Christ's love.

Testimony: The Reverend Cari Pattison

For the past eight years, the Reverend Cari Pattison has served as Associate Pastor of The Reformed Church of Bronxville, New York. Prior to that, she served part-time for three years at Praise Presbyterian Church in Somerset, New Jersey. She has worked in youth ministry, hospital chaplaincy, college campus ministry, and summer camp counseling.

I grew up in the church and in a Christian family, and cannot recall a time I did not know about Jesus' love, and the power of God. From a young age I was deeply interested in the world beyond what I could see and touch, and had an intuitive longing toward connection through prayer. My formative faith experiences ranged from Sunday school to various camps and youth group trips. I was influenced by a handful of mentors who nurtured me and took seriously my spiritual questions.

In college I became closely involved with Intervarsity Christian Fellowship and began leading small group Bible studies and service projects. This was really my first entrée into evangelical Christianity, along with varieties of Pentecostalism. On Sundays I would visit various churches and wonder whether I wanted to stay in my Reformed denomination, or move toward Catholicism, non-denominational evangelicalism, or another mainline Protestant denomination.

A real turning point in those early, young-adult years came when I spent my junior year of college abroad in Nairobi, Kenya. I experienced church there on a whole different level with a congregation called Nairobi Chapel, which was full of vibrant youth, energy, dancing, and lively music. Amazed at how the same gospel, Bible, and Jesus could be just as alive—if not more so!—halfway across the globe, I felt deep confirmation in my Christian convictions. I was especially moved by my Kenyan friends' commitment to prayer, and their ability to laugh at life's challenges, a kind of "holy hilarity," Richard Foster calls it.

It was the first time I honestly considered that I could do ministry as a full time vocation. However, I had friends in my Christian college fellowship who thought that 1 Timothy, Ephesians, and 1 Corinthians expressly prohibited women from speaking and teaching in church and having leadership over men. I had never been raised with these interpretations, but neither did the large Presbyterian church of my youth have prominent women leaders or preachers.

This was a genuine hurdle for me, but one that strong mentors and role models talked me through and encouraged me out of. Especially impactful for me was the example of a woman pastor at my church in Nairobi. While the Kenyan culture is more conservative overall, the church nevertheless recognized Pastor Janet's leadership gifts and preaching. After college I returned to Nairobi Chapel and served for a year as an intern, serving in various capacities and preaching sermons to youth and college students. I loved it. I felt creative, engaged, and in awe of how I sensed God working through me. I enjoyed the feedback and conversation from people afterward, learning what the Scripture and sermon stirred up for them. I realized the impact that both preaching and thoughtful pastoral leadership can have on people at so many crucial stages of their lives.

When I returned from Kenya, I used my degree to teach eighth grade English for a year. Although I enjoyed teaching, I longed to go deeper with the kids, to get to know them and their families, and to help them develop over time, none of which public school teaching really allows. I decided my instincts in Kenya were right, and that seminary would be my next move. I looked at two different seminaries, and decided on the one that returned me to my Reformed roots, after many years of exploring the Catholic and evangelical streams of Christian faith.

Unlike a number of my peers, I did not have a clear sense that parish ministry would be my call. I thought I might graduate from seminary and become a chaplain, professor, or missionary. However, my field education experiences in churches and hospitals were formative in pointing me toward congregational ministry for my initial call.

When I first came to Bronxville, where I now pastor, it was honestly more out of necessity for a job than it was a strong sense of "Oh-my-gosh-God's-calling-me-here!" Yet what I have discovered since being here has been one, long, surprising journey of growing into a call. It never ceases to amaze me how much I love being a parish minister, getting to know families and individuals over time, and being there with them in life's key moments, from birth to death, marriage to divorce, baptism to confirmation, joy to sorrow. I love that I get to preach regularly, teach youth, lead Bible studies, and meet with people for counsel and prayer. It is a privilege to have such a fulfilling and varied job that allows me to share with others the good news of hope in Jesus Christ.

For Reflection

1. Reflect on whether you think Scripture alone informs our view of women in ministry? How might cultural and societal views of gender roles impact our view of women in ministry?

2. Consider your own childhood home. How were gender roles viewed in the home where you grew up? Who was in charge of making the decisions about moving, disciplining children, and money? Who worked outside of the home?

3

Scripture & Women in Ministry

CAN WE BE CONFIDENT THAT
SCRIPTURE POINTS TO GOD?

The church has affirmed the role of Scripture in shaping all aspects of the life and work of the individual believer and church universal. Scripture introduces us to life with God, and its authority comes from the adherence of its subject matter to the revelation of God in Christ. Even more than that, when we take a relational approach to understanding Scripture, we recognize that God speaks to us in and through the Bible.

Scripture is not self-interpreting. Therefore, it is both useful and enriching for the church when faithful interpreters, constrained by the rule of faith, provide fresh and insightful interpretations.[1] Faithful interpreters probably will not come up with the exact same meaning from a text of Scripture as what was originally intended by the author or understood by the ancient readers. Times and places have changed dramatically. The Spirit brings fresh meaning for new readers. Certainly, "imagination is required by the interpreter to exploit more easily the inherent multivalency of biblical teaching in order to find new meanings for new

---

1. Wall, "Reading the Bible from within Our Traditions," 97.

worlds."[2] Within the boundaries of the church's rule of faith, there is a range of possible meanings faithful interpreters take from the text to deliver the subject matter in meaningful ways.[3]

IS IT AS SIMPLE AS JUST "BELIEVING WHAT THE BIBLE SAYS" ABOUT WOMEN IN MINISTRY?

"We believe what the Bible says!" This confession, often voiced by Protestant evangelicals, echoes the Reformation's appeal to *sola Scriptura* to settle disagreements over matters of faith and practice. Sometimes believers appeal to Scripture's authority without recognizing that "what the Bible says" has as much to do with the sociology and theology a particular interpreter brings to the text as with what one finds in the text itself. Nevermind the reality that no one really lives out everything the Bible says or that the goal is to hear not what the Bible says but what God is speaking in and through the Bible. In truth, "our supposed listening is in fact a strange mixture of hearing and our own speaking."[4] This "strange mixture" is not brewed magically from within ourselves. We come to Scripture with certain religious beliefs, culturally based preferences, and personal experiences in mind. This means that we are always picking and choosing certain things and not others from the Bible. While this can be disconcerting to some, the question to ask is how can we do our *inevitable* selective picking and choosing in a way that takes God seriously and upholds Scripture as God's authoritative word in every time and place. Further, we would do well to remember that God freely chooses to speak to us through the biblical word in light of who we are and where we are. This means that rather than pursuing one correct interpretation of each text, as though God intended only one meaning to be found, believers constantly learn new things from Scripture in dynamic cooperation with the Spirit.

2. Wall, "Canonical Context," 174.

3. Ibid.

4. Ibid.

The reason we are able to learn new things from Scripture stems from the very being and character of God. God is not static. God is alive, and at work in our world. God has spoken to the church through Scripture in every day and age, but the Spirit does not take us back to a past moment in time when God was at work in a different time and place only to end up saying the same thing in the same way today. Instead, God is more than capable of saying fresh things in our day that speak into our culture and are specific to our social location. Of course this does not mean that we can ignore what God has said and done in the past. Quite the contrary, we ought to learn from and respect what God has done throughout history. Learning from and respecting the ways that God has empowered the gospel message to speak into other cultures, past ages, and different languages, however, does not mean that we stay stuck at those other, past, and different ways that God has made the biblical word come alive. In fact, faithful Christian interpreters who have gone before us, whether biblical authors or past church leaders, went back to Scripture (not tradition) in order to move forward into their context. By going back to Scripture, they and we allow the Spirit the freedom to continue to renew who we are, what we think, and how we live by the biblical word.[5]

Katherine Zell: 1497–1562

Katherine was born in Germany and, by the age of seven, wanted to find out about God. By the time she was ten years old she had learned to weave picture tapestries, a trade dominated by women. She supported herself completely. Matthew Zell, a Catholic priest, wanted to marry her and form a ministry partnership with their marriage. On these terms they were married, and Matthew commissioned her to serve refugees and the poor. The Catholic church ex-communicated Matthew for his marriage, but the Lutheran church took him in. When rumors of their marriage began to hurt his ministry, Katherine wrote and published a well-argued biblical

5. For more on this topic, see McKnight, *The Blue Parakeet*, 22–37.

defense for their marriage. Later it was commended by Martin Luther. Katherine continued her theological writing and corresponded with various religious reformers of the day. When Matthew died in 1548, Katherine began preaching in his place. She was a comfort to many people. She preached about the righteousness of Christ, who is the true Good Shepherd. She also spoke out against the Catholic church, published songs for children, presided over funerals, and was in charge of choosing new pastors for Lutheran congregations.

How does Scripture Portray Faithful Women in Successful Ministry?

Scripture is full of examples, throughout the Old and New Testaments, of faithful women leading and ministering to God's people. In the Old Testament, God often uses women in somewhat subtle and subversive ways. They are resourceful and wise risk-takers. In many narratives, they are the ones who speak with the most clarity about God. Women in the New Testament are followers and ministers of Jesus and key figures in the early church. They participate in the growth of Christianity in many ways, including prophesying and teaching. Biblical portraits of faithful women in ministry are helpful because they help spark our imaginations as we deal with contemporary issues of women in the church.[6]

How Should We Think about the Varying Pictures of Women throughout Scripture?

When we think about this question, it is helpful to remember that the Christian leaders who decided on the final form and order of the canon (complete collection of the books) of Christian Scripture used a particular logic. For example, it is not by happenstance that the New Testament is sequentially placed after the

6. For a helpful and concise review of women throughout Scripture see, "Women Characters in Scripture," in LaCelle-Peterson, *Liberating Tradition*.

Old Testament or that the New Testament begins with the gospel accounts of Jesus' life and ministry rather than with Paul's letter to the church in Rome. Each unit of the New Testament (gospel, acts, letters, and apocalypse) "is assigned a specific role to perform within the whole, which in turn offers another explanation for the rich diversity of theology, literature, and language that casts Scripture's subject matter."[7] The four Gospels are placed first in the New Testament to emphasize the importance of the story of what Jesus said and did. This is an underlying guide for all the writings that follow it in the New Testament. In the same way, the book of Acts is a narrative of the apostles of Jesus. Following Pentecost, they were to be Jesus' successors to spread the gospel to all the ends of the earth. Acts serves as an introduction to the letters of these apostles, which form a great portion of the New Testament. Therefore, when we go to different biblical texts featuring women, it is important to keep in mind the section of Scripture where the text is found. For example, since the book of Acts tells the story of how the new Christian church began to spread the gospel far and wide, women featured in the book of Acts particularly emphasize the important role women play in the mission of the church. By the same token, when Paul includes greetings to female church leaders in his letters, we learn that since its beginning, the church has been strengthened by leadership from both men and women.

Bible Study and Discussion Questions

Read Ex 2:1–25

1. List the women in this story.

2. How are the women resourceful?

3. Compare and contrast the women to the men in this text.

4. Does anything surprise you about Moses' birth, character, and personality?

---

7. Wall, "Canonical Context," 175.

Read Luke 1:5–56

1. Describe the women in this story according to the details about them in the text. What do you notice?

2. Compare and contrast the women to the men in this text.

3. What is the theme of Mary's praise to God in verses 45–46?

4. What do you notice about the biblical portrait of women in the Lukan and Exodus texts?

5. Do you see any "logic" in the order and placement of these two stories in Scripture both in terms of their place in the Old and New Testaments and their location in texts recounting the birth of two major biblical figures (Moses and Jesus)?

For Reflection

1. What role has Scripture played in your life?

2. What value can be gained from keeping in mind the whole sweep of Scripture as well as looking closely at specific contexts of any passage of Scripture?

3. How does who you are and where you live shape how you understand Scripture? Think of specific examples.

HOW ARE WOMEN LEADERS PORTRAYED IN THE OLD TESTAMENT?

It is important to recognize just how powerful are the stories about women in the Old Testament. They are powerful because stories impact how we understand who we are. For Jewish and Christian women alike, these stories contribute to how we view ourselves. Likewise, for men, these stories impact perceptions about women. Old Testament stories about women, as you might well be thinking, are not all positive portrayals, nor are they all about woman leaders. Whole books have been written exploring the many and varied female characters, named and unnamed, in the Old Testament. Some of the stories about women focus, positively or negatively, on their familial roles, which were the most basic roles women had in ancient Israel, roles as wives, sisters, daughters, and mothers. Still other stories show women in roles as prostitutes or victims of harm, whether sexual, physical, or otherwise. Finally, we have Old Testament stories about women that clearly portray them as heroes of some sort or another. Kristina LaCelle-Peterson has come up with six categories for women figures in the Old Testament: women who conversed with God, women who sacrificed to protect men, other women who were victimized, negative examples of powerful women, redeemer figures, and prophets.[8] All of these categories and various stories of women in the Old Testament are worth considering in full in relationship to the question of women in ministry. We will consider just a few pertinent examples here.

Deborah

Deborah was both a judge and a prophet. The judges of Israel were chosen for their outstanding leadership gifts. They were to make God's justice and compassion known to Israel. Prophets of Israel spoke on behalf of God to the people. Except for Abraham in Gen 20:7, Deborah is the first person to be called a prophet in Israel's story. Under her leadership, the land had rest for forty years. Deborah was one of the last good judges of Israel. She was also a poet. She crafted a song extolling God's holiness, power, and faithfulness to Israel. Deborah is the only person in Scripture to combine the role of leader, judge, prophet, and poet.

Bible Study and Discussion Questions

Read Judges 4–5

The cast of characters in this account includes:

8. See LaCelle-Peterson, *Liberating Tradition*, 43–55.

- Deborah: judge and prophet
- Barak: general of the Israelite forces
- Jabin: King of Canaan and oppressor of the Israelites
- Sisera: general of King Jabin's armies
- Jael: wife of Heber the Kenite, slayer of Sisera
- Sisera's unnamed mother

In Judges, a pattern emerges showing the relationship between Israel and God through Israel's disobedience, God's provision of a deliverer, Israel's period of rest, and, finally, Israel's fall into disobedience once again. The pattern in Judges 4 centers on God's provision of a deliverer for Israel.

For Reflection

How do the women in Judges 4–5 act on God's behalf as unconventional deliverers for Israel?

Huldah

Huldah was a prophet of Israel. She lived in "the house of doctrine" near the temple and was among the learned, those who gathered to search the Scriptures together. When Josiah found the Book of the Law, he commanded the priest to take it to Huldah. She inquired of the Lord for Josiah. Huldah spoke on behalf of the Lord to Israel and proclaimed God's judgment and mercy to them.

Bible Study and Discussion Questions

Read 2 Kings 22

1. What is the significance of the Book of the Law for Israel?
2. Why is it important that the Book of the Law was found?

3. In your own words, describe the word of the Lord that Huldah brought to the priest.

Esther

The book of Esther tells the fascinating and fast-paced story of Esther's rise to royalty as a queen and her risky plan to save the Jewish people from utter destruction by her husband, the Persian king Ahasuerus (Xerxes I). The arc of Esther's story moves from her beginnings as a passive young woman who is taken from her adoptive father and placed in the king's harem to her end in triumph as an influential leader who successfully navigates a corrupt political system and risks her own life in order to enact salvation for her people. While many who read the book note its lack of any reference to God, it is important to remember that the book assumes God's control of events and the Jews as God's chosen people. Also notable, at the opening of the book, is the story of Queen Vashti's banishment by the king because of her own steadfast refusal to parade naked (wearing only her royal crown!) before the drunken king and all of his equally intoxicated party guests. Old Testament scholar Katharine Doob Sakenfeld has suggested that the stories of Vashti and Esther provide us with two different "models of resistance to wrong: Vashti exercised personal direct dissent that led to her banishment and efforts at further societal repression; Esther worked 'within the system,' even using feminine wiles, as a strategy for saving herself and others."[9] We do not need to choose one model over another; instead it is helpful to reflect on the advantages and risks of both models. For women in positions of power, specific tactics are not the most important consideration when the end goal is the promotion of justice, mercy, and peace. "Over the long haul, a variety of approaches to challenging the status quo will be needed."[10]

9. Sakenfeld, *Just Wives?*, 64.
10. Ibid., 65.

Bible Study and Discussion Questions

Read Vashti's story in Esther 1 and Esther's story in Esther 2 and 7–8

1. Consider whether your own leadership approach is more like Vashti (standing up against systems you disapprove of) or Esther (working within the system) and how your approach may differ depending on the circumstances or issues being confronted.

2. In your experience, are there times when physical appearance impacts the degree to which a woman is able to be effective or successful in ministry or the workplace? What do you think about this?[11]

Wisdom

Wisdom is the counter-testimony given to Israel when God is silent. Wisdom is personified as a woman. All people are to heed Wisdom (Prov 8:10–11). Wisdom is also the image of God's goodness to all creation. Wisdom was with God before the creation of the world. Wisdom sustains all things and offers life and rest to those who accept her. In the New Testament, we begin to see parallels between Wisdom and Jesus.

Bible Study and Discussion Questions

Read Prov 1–9 and 31:10–31

1. According to Prov 1:2–6, what is the purpose of the book of Proverbs?

2. According to Prov 1:7 and 9:10, what is the relationship between the worship of God and Wisdom?

11. Ibid., 66.

3. According to Prov 3:13–18, how is Wisdom personified?

4. What does Wisdom give to those who embrace her?

5. According to Prov 8:1–36, how is Wisdom personified?

6. What are the qualities of Wisdom?

7. When was Wisdom created?

8. What was her role in the creation of the world (See also Prov 3:19–20)?

9. What is the basic message of Prov 8:34–36?

10. According to Prov 31:10–31, how does the "ideal wife" spend her days?

Testimony: Jennifer Herold

Jennifer's first "official" ministry experience was in 2011–2012 when she served as an intern with the INN University Ministries in Bellingham, Washington. It was there that she fell in love with college ministry and felt God calling her to seminary to learn more about her specific call to ordained ministry. Since then, she has completed her first year at Princeton Theological Seminary and plans to graduate with a dual MDiv/MSW degree, thereby combining her passion for the ministries of counseling and social justice.

Only a few years ago, I never would have pictured myself attending seminary and working toward a career in the church. Growing up in an atheist family, I had almost no exposure to Christianity. When I found Christ in high school, I had no background or family support to help me understand my new faith. I resorted to books, Christian friends, and the skewed perception of Christianity that I had picked up from media portrayals. Even as an insecure high school student, I held on to my feminist and egalitarian understanding of gender roles, but I could not reconcile those strongly held beliefs with what Christian culture told me about my relationships with men and myself. I had to mentally separate my religious life, with its expectations of submissiveness and chastity, from every other aspect, including my intellectual and emotional life.

I was never exposed to women preaching in a formal setting, yet in small ways I began to get a taste of informal ministry, beginning my senior year of high school and continuing throughout college. I learned to plan services, lead Bible studies, and as I did so, I fell deeply in love with studying the Bible. At my secular, state university, I took elective courses on the Hebrew Bible and the New Testament, relishing the challenges that my nonreligious peers and professor brought to my faith and understanding of God. I found that I had gifts for ministry, particularly in pastoral care, which were valuable to my congregation. Still, it never even occurred to me that I could do all of these things that I loved in a professional capacity. As far as I could tell, the essential work of ministry was preaching, and I had a panic-inducing fear of public speaking. Even if I could contribute to a few aspects of church life, someone more competent than me, and, of course, someone male, would do the "real" ministry.

Around that time, I began dating someone from my high school youth group. He grew up in a family with narrowly defined gender roles, and had attended a Christian college that only perpetuated that mindset. We dated for two years, and in that time I became resigned, even accustomed, to being the submissive Christian girlfriend-turned-future-wife. However, my excitement about studying the Bible and my new interest in ministry led me to consider a post-graduation college ministry internship. As a student I had been encouraged and affirmed in my leadership, and so, as I neared the end of college, I began to consider the possibility that God might be calling me to explore ministry as a profession. I vividly remember a phone conversation with my boyfriend in which I excitedly told him about this internship opportunity and brought up, timidly, the possibility that I might attend seminary. His response was crushing: he told me that he disliked the idea that his future wife would be more knowledgeable about the Bible than he was, and besides, I did not like speaking in public, so how could I possibly be a pastor?

I was devastated, and, for a few months, I believed and internalized his words. Fortunately, God rebuilt my confidence through the support of friends and mentors, and I not only applied for the ministry internship and was accepted, but also ended that toxic relationship. My internship year was one of great growth and challenges as I planned services, events, and mission trips, led groups of volunteers, and sat across coffee shop tables listening to students share their stories. I knew that there was no way that God was going to let me continue my life on the trajectory I had planned. The following year I applied for seminary and was accepted. I moved across the country to begin my first year, with few plans for the future, but great excitement for the next few years in school and whatever God has for me after graduation.

One Christmas break, I returned home from my first semester of seminary. Several extended family members asked me, incredulously, what exactly I am doing with my life. As I explained what seminary is and what I expect to do in my future ministry, one uncle asked, brow furrowed, "Are you even allowed to do that?" Once that question might have been confusing, or even hurtful. Now, after a semester of seminary education and with new confidence that God has called me to this, I was able to laugh it off and answer, "Yes. I most definitely am."

For Reflection

1. Are you or do you know a woman pursuing a call to ministry? What has been your/her experience?
2. Reflect on how a lack of understanding and support from family, close friends, and significant others might impact one's call.

Teresa of Avila: 1515–1582

Teresa was born in Avila, Spain. Her mother died when she was fifteen years old. Her father saw that she needed motherly guidance and entrusted her to the Augustian nuns at Santa Maria de

Gracia. Teresa rediscovered her early childhood piety and, in 1535, entered the Carmelite Monastery of the Incarnation at Avila. She gave herself over completely to the work of prayer and penance. She soon became very ill and almost died. Her father brought her home, and she entered into a coma so deep she was thought to be dead. After four days she revived, but as a result her legs were paralyzed for three years. Following this experience, Teresa went through a time of mediocrity in her spiritual life, yet she did not give up praying. For the next eighteen years, she had transitory mystical experiences. At the age of thirty-nine, she had a dramatic experience of the presence of the image of Christ badly wounded. After that, she began to enjoy a deep sense of God's presence within her. She struggled in the incarnation monastery, wanting desperately to perfectly keep the rules of monastic life but finding the atmosphere to be less than ideal. This was the start of her vocation in establishing new monastic orders. The first one, in 1562, was called the order of the Discalced Carmelites. In 1567, the Carmelite general commissioned Teresa to establish other convents as well as two houses for men who wished to adopt the Carmelite reform. During this time in her life, Teresa wrote several books that set out her doctrine of prayer and instructions to the new orders. In her book, *The Interior Castle*, she wrote of the soul as the interior castle in which dwells the Trinity. By growing in prayer, individuals are able to have deeper communion with God. When an individual has attained the highest degree of union with God permitted in this world, she has reached her own inward center and thus has great integrity as both a child of God and a human being.

How are Faithful Women Portrayed in Relationship to Jesus?

Considering the cultural customs of his day, Jesus' treatment of women was scandalous. Jesus taught women in private, a privilege reserved for male students. He spoke directly with women and publicly socialized with them. Jesus shared theological truth with women. In his stories and parables, women were protagonists.

Jesus even used a woman character to represent God. Jesus healed and touched women, and he let them touch him. During his crucifixion, women were some of the only friends who stayed with Jesus, and they were the first to see the risen Lord and proclaim the resurrection to the rest of Jesus' disciples.

Women were vital to Jesus' ministry and key followers (Luke 8:1–3; Mark 15:40–41; Matt 27:55–56). They were included among those who traveled with Jesus as disciples. These women had to break Jewish custom to leave their homes and travel publicly with Jesus. Luke takes the time to mention a few of the many women by name—indicating their importance among the disciples of Jesus. Women provided for Jesus out of their own resources. Some scholars think that these women might have even provided the financial resources Jesus needed.

Bible Study and Discussion Questions

Read Luke 8:1–3; 23:49, 55–56; 24:1; 8:21

1. List the women included with Jesus and the Twelve.

2. Compare Luke 8:21 to the other Lukan passages listed above. What is the connection between Jesus' call to ministry and natural responsibilities given by sex?

3. What do we learn about Jesus' vision of discipleship from these texts?

The Samaritan Woman

A few things can be said specifically about the interaction between Jesus and the Samaritan woman in John 4:4–42. From the beginning of their conversation to its end, the discussion is deeply theological, and the woman questions "Jesus on virtually every significant tenet of Samaritan theology. . . . She is a genuine theological dialogue partner gradually experiencing Jesus' self-revelation even as she reveals herself to him."[12] Also, like the apostles in the Synoptic Gospels, whose abandonment of daily life to follow Jesus is symbolized by their leaving of such things as nets, boats, tax stalls, or parents, this woman leaves behind her ordinary life to evangelize her town. This is symbolized by leaving behind her water jar.[13]

There are three key aspects to how women are portrayed in John. The first is the self-revelation of Jesus to women. Jesus' self-revelation to the Samaritan woman as the Messiah is given in the "I am" formula. This formula is very significant in John, and its first appearance is in the story of the Samaritan woman. The second important aspect in John is the role women have as witnesses. The Samaritan woman's witness to her own town is extremely noteworthy. Those who hear her "come to him" (4:30), which is John's expression for the first movement of saving faith in Jesus (see 6:37). That her witness was fully effective is indicated by the Samaritans coming to faith in Jesus as the Savior of the world. "This woman is the first and only person (presented) in the public life of Jesus through whose word of witness a group of people is brought to 'come and see' and 'to believe in Jesus.'"[14] The final aspect of the Johannine presentation of women is the discomfort of Jesus' male disciples. When the disciples find Jesus talking with the Samaritan woman, they are shocked by Jesus' dialogue with her but say nothing about it. This curious little detail of their silent shock serves to vindicate the Samaritan woman's "discipleship, apostleship, and ministry in the face of the cultural patterns that might have challenged its appropriateness or even legitimacy."[15]

12. Schneiders, *Written That You May Believe*, 139, 141.

13. Ibid., 141.

14. Ibid., 142.

15. Ibid., 104.

Bible Study and Discussion Questions

Read John 4:4–42; 3:1–21

1. In what ways is the story of the Samaritan woman like the episode with Nicodemus?

2. In what ways is it different?

3. Summarize the flow of the conversation Jesus has with the Samaritan woman.

4. What do you notice about the conversation?

Read John 4:16–19; Hosea 1:1; 2:1–7

1. In light of the verses in Hosea, what is interesting about the Samaritan woman's designation of Jesus as a prophet?

For Reflection

Why do you think that Christian readings of the story often put so much focus on the marital situation of the woman and usually ignore that the story ends with the woman's vindication in her role as an apostle?

How Does the Picture of Women Leaders in Acts Shape Paul's Instructions for Women?

Peter's explanation of Pentecost, using the prophecy from Joel, indicates that a new day has dawned for humanity. It is a time when the things said and done by followers of Jesus take on even greater importance. In this new day of God's Spirit, there are no longer any customary boundaries to restrict the Spirit's outpouring on some and not others. In other words, there is no gender, age, or class discrimination within this Spirit-filled community. All people will receive God's Spirit and speak like prophets. The outcome is nothing less than the salvation of all who call on the Lord (Acts 2:21). The inclusivity of the Spirit means that the entire church (male and female, young and old, slave and free) is invited to be a part of the community of faith's new vocation as witnesses to the resurrected Jesus.

For Reflection

1. How important was Pentecost to the church?

2. What do you take from the inclusion of both men and women in the Spirit's empowerment to prophesy?

Elizabeth Fry: 1780–1865

Elizabeth was born in Norfolk, England to a Quaker family. As a child, she found Quakers boring and would wear purple boots to church to liven things up. It was a visiting preacher, a friend of the family, who got Elizabeth's attention. As God changed her heart, she found she no longer struggled with her love for the pleasures of the world but wanted to be a preacher for those who did. She joined the strictest sect of the Society of Friends and found their meetings beautiful. She met older women who were preachers and prophetesses who inspired her. One of those women, Deborah Darby, saw Elizabeth's desire to honor God and thought she should be a minister for Christ. Elizabeth began teaching Quaker children. It was soon discovered that she had a great gift. At her father's graveside service Elizabeth spoke to those in attendance. She felt the holy Spirit come upon her and prayed out loud. This was the start of her ministry. She began visiting women prisoners. She was not afraid of the bad conditions of the prisons, focusing instead on serving the women and advocating for prison reform. She went on ships transporting convicts and ministered to them, instituting libraries and schools on the ships and teaching the prisoners how to make clothes that they could sell. Elizabeth had an influence on Florence

Nightingale who was a "Fry Nurse." Fry Nurses cared for patients' physical and spiritual needs.

Priscilla

The story of Priscilla's ministry in Acts 18 introduces us to the Pauline passages that instruct Christian women to submit as good wives and mothers (cf. Eph 5:21–24; 1 Cor 7:34–35), to remain silent as good students (cf. 1 Tim 2:9–12; 1 Cor 14:34), and to circumscribe their prophetic ministry by head coverings (cf. 1 Cor 11:2–10). In the story of Priscilla, all of these issues are addressed. In Acts 18, Priscilla has an equitable partnership with her husband in both the workplace (18:2) and the local congregation (18:26), and even takes the lead in these efforts (18:18). She is also able to instruct a Christian man more accurately in the way of the Lord (18:26). While the above-stated Pauline passages give negative instructions to women, the portrait of Priscilla is very positive and, in a way, relativizes the influence of any one Pauline text as a moral norm. Priscilla's story more closely resembles the gospel witness of Jesus' interactions with women disciples and follows another Pauline teaching about women: that "in Christ" gender categories of male and female no longer apply as structural boundaries. (Gal 3:28).

Bible Study and Discussion Questions

Read Acts 2:17–22; 18:24–28

One theme in Acts is the constant unfolding of the implications of the prophecy in Joel quoted by Peter in Acts 2. Acts 18:24–28 is an example of the implications of the Spirit's indiscriminate empowerment. One way that the Spirit is manifested in people's lives in Acts is in their ability to interpret Scripture in light of who Jesus is.

1. What do you notice about the description of Apollos in 18:24–25?

2. List the factors of Apollos' ministry in 18:27–28.

3. What is the turning point for Apollos between these two passages?

For Reflection

What effect does the portrait of Priscilla in Acts 18:24–28 and the impact she had on the life and ministry of Apollos have on your thoughts on women's full participation in all forms of ministry leadership?

What do the Pauline Letters Tell Us about the Important Place of Women within the Ministry of the Church?

Galatians

Galatians 3:28 sums up much of what is emphasized in various ways throughout the Pauline letters. In Christ there is equality among what society and religious tradition have previously deemed irreconcilable distinctions. Men and women are equal in Christ. Paul seems to suggest that being "in Christ" is more essential than one's gender. The old way of creating boundaries and limitations based on our differences from one another do not stand up in the Christian community. We have a new identity in Jesus Christ that brings freedom where once there were limits imposed because of our social, economic, and gender identity.

For Reflection

What do you imagine was the impact of Galatians 3:28 on churches in Paul's day, considering the cultural norms of the ancient world?

Romans

In Romans 16, the end of Paul's great letter to the Roman Christians, he lists a number of church leaders by name. These twenty-six individuals are persons worthy of his praise. Nine of those mentioned are women. The list begins with Phoebe, whom Paul mentions is a deacon of the church in Cenchreae. "Many translate the word as 'deaconess,' but the word itself is masculine, the same word used elsewhere in the New Testament for that office."[16] This suggests that she held the same responsibilities in her position as a man. Paul also praises the wife and husband team Prisca and Aquila, noting that they are his coworkers in Christ (16:3–4). Biblical scholars have noted that "Paul used the name Prisca, rather than its diminutive form [a word formed from another by the addition of a suffix and expressing smallness in size or condescension] Priscilla, in referring to her, and that in his greetings he places her name before that of Aquila her husband."[17] Among other women praised in this text is Junia, who, along with her husband, Andronicus, is a standout among the apostles (16:7). Junia's story, however, extends beyond the closing words in Romans. From the beginning of the church, it was understood that Junia and Andronicus were a ministry couple like Prisca and Aquila. However, a man named Aegidius of Rome (1245–1316), believing that women could not be apostles, added an "s" to the end of Junia's name, making it appear to be a masculine name (Junias not Junia). However, his interpretive decision is not supported by the Greek texts of the New Testament and recent scholarship has demonstrated that there is no support in Greek literature for the masculine name "Junias," whereas "Junia" was a common female name.[18]

---

16. Bristow, *What Paul Really Said about Women*, 57.

17. Ibid.

18. LaCelle-Peterson, *Liberating Tradition*, 63–64.

For Reflection

1. Read through Romans 16 and consider what the activities of the women might imply for women in ministry today.

2. Why might it be important that the women in Romans 16 are described with phrases that are used in other New Testament texts to describe men in leadership positions in the church?

3. Why do you think these women co-workers of Paul are often overlooked?

1 Corinthians[19]

Out of all of Paul's letters 1 Corinthians has the most to say not only about gender but also sexuality, making our investigation into 1 Corinthians 11 especially helpful for our study on the question of women in ministry. But even a cursory reading of 11:2–16 tells us that the particular congregation being addressed by Paul was probably *overly* zealous in their efforts to live out his new creation teaching, relating, and serving one another as male and female. They were taking too far (imagine such a thing!) Paul's insistence that Christ's death and resurrection have inaugurated a new age in the midst of the old world and transformed how we are to be the people of God in the world. Paul wants the church to demonstrate the reality of the new creation by living as a new, inclusive community of God and sharing in the ministry of reconciliation. This ministry of reconciliation proceeds on the new basis that "in Christ" the categories of race, social standing, and gender are irrelevant as structural boundaries (Gal 3:28). This is the heartbeat of Paul's message throughout his letters. Yet, while it is important to acknowledge that there is not a lot of certainty about the exact cultural and church context of the Corinthian congregation, it appears that some women in the Corinthian congregation were

19. What follows is a revised and condensed version of Smythe, "Gender Reconciliation."

disregarding customary distinctions between the sexes when they prayed and prophesied in worship.

Let's be clear here: the problem was not that women were leading in worship along with men by praying and prophesying, but the manner in which they were doing so. So eager were they to lean into Paul's new creation teaching that they were somehow acting as if there were no actual gender differences among them. For such a notoriously difficult passage to fully understand, it is a travesty that 1 Cor 11:2–16 has so often been used to promote the subordination of women to men within both church and home.[20] Not only does such an interpretation mean the very converse of Paul's words to the Corinthian congregation (1 Cor 11:10–12), it also requires an equally opposite understanding of Paul's new creation theology in general, including the teachings of 2 Cor 5:14–20 and Gal 3:26–28.

Paul's response to the women's behavior consists of three different arguments aimed at addressing the behavior of the Corinthian women. The first argument (1 Cor 11:2–6) trades on cultural ideas of honor and shame; the second (1 Cor 11:7–12) on the creation order; and the third (1 Cor 11:13–16) on what is proper and customary. Each argument supports Paul's recommendation that the women have some sort of covering on their head when praying and prophesying in church. Again, let's not forget that Paul wants them to continue to pray and prophesy in worship. Yet, as odd as it might seem to us, he has some thoughts on what they choose to wear in worship. What Paul really wants to convey to the Corinthians, as he specifically addresses the women's attire in worship, is that women and men have a relational responsibility to one another rather than just individual freedom in how they dress for worship.

In Paul's first argument, he works with typical cultural notions in that day regarding honor and shame. In essence, Paul wants to

20. Interpretations that take this line disregard completely the fact that nothing in the text says a word about women being subjected to men. Such readings are based on a faulty reading of "head" (*kephalē*) in verse 3 as meaning "authority" rather than the more likely metaphorical meaning "source" as in "source of life."

uphold that there are still sexual distinctions in the new creation community. Gender neutrality is not an option. "By making their appearance such that it tended to eliminate distinctions between the sexes, they [the women] were bringing shame on that relationship, which has not yet been abrogated even though the new age had been inaugurated."[21] This is not to say that Paul is here setting up a hierarchical pattern (hierarchy is only introduced into the passage by translating the Greek word *kephalē* as "authority"[22]), but to highlight another important element throughout his letters, which is his continual insistence on mutual submission (Eph 5:18–33; Phil 2:1–11; Gal 5:20–33; Rom 15:1–3; 1 Cor 6–7; 10:24, 33; 14:34–40).

Looking closer at the finer points of Paul's first argument, we can see that he is corroborating his statement in 11:3 that man is the head (source) of woman with his allusion in 11:8 and 11:12 to the creation accounts from Genesis 1 and 2. Second, we find that his point that Christ is the head (source) of every man fits well with his statement in 2 Cor 5:17 that a person is a new creation as a result of being in Christ. We need to be careful in our conclusions from 11:3 because, while Paul did not include women in this statement of being in Christ, neither did he rule it out. On this matter, Gordon Fee counsels that Paul is not, in these verses, setting out a comprehensive theological statement on men and women and their relationship to Christ, God, and each other. Instead, he is trying to construct an argument to support what he says about men's attire in worship in 11:4. Finally, we would do well to remember that when Paul writes that God is the head (source) of Christ (11:3), he is not thinking of the ontological dynamics of Christology and the Trinity. That would be to make Paul into an

---

21. Fee, *The First Epistle to the Corinthians*, 502. My discussion of this text rests heavily on the careful and respected work of Fee in his magisterial commentary on 1 Corinthians.

22. To understand Paul's metaphorical use of head (*kephalē*) in 1 Cor 11:3–5 to mean "authority" not only contradicts all normal classical and contemporary Greek usage of the word, but also ignores the immediate textual parameters.

early church systematic theologian, which he is not. Paul is referring to the incarnational work of Christ, whose source is God.

To summarize, Paul's first argument is concerned that there not be a dismissal of sexual distinctions in Christian worship.[23] In his second argument, which works with ideas about the creation order (1 Cor 11:7–12), Paul highlights that the woman is the man's glory. Yet even as he says this, remember that he never says anything to deny that woman too was made in the image of God and is also the glory of God. Furthermore, Paul "says nothing about man's authority; his concern is with the woman's being man's *glory*, the one without whom he is not complete (vv. 7c–9)."[24] But, what does it mean for the woman to be man's glory? A good suggestion is that Paul is further reflecting on the Genesis texts to which he alludes (see Gen 2:18–20, 23). He echoes Genesis in the idea that the man needs a suitable helper so that he will not be alone. The man needs someone who is like him but different from him. That someone is the woman whom God creates from his rib. Upon discovering her, the man literally "glories" in her through song, recognizing not that she is his subordinate, but that he needs her in order to be complete.[25]

Turning to 11:11–12, we can see that it is almost as if Paul knows that his words in 11:8–9 might be misunderstood by the Corinthians to mean a woman's subordination to a man. But what the Corinthians will notice about Paul's argument in the Greek, which we often miss in the English, is that the sentences in 11:11–12 are written by Paul in such a way that they line up perfectly with the wording he uses in 11:8–9. This signals to the Corinthians that there is a limit to the applicability of 11:8–9. First Corinthians 11:11–12 again supports Paul's main point throughout this passage: that women and men have a relational responsibility to one

---

23. For all the time Paul devotes to his arguments in this matter, his style of argumentation is much less intense than in 11:17–34. This suggests that while distinctions between the sexes are to be maintained, "for Paul it does not seem to be a life-and-death matter" (Fee, *The First Epistle to the Corinthians*, 530).

24. Ibid., 503–4.

25. Ibid., 517.

another rather than just individual freedom in how they dress for worship. Furthermore, if Paul's prior allusion in 11:7–8 was to the creation story in Genesis 2, now, in 11:11–12, he widens the allusion to include not only Gen 1:26–28 but also possibly Gen 4:1. Again, these allusions serve Paul's theological point in regards to women's head coverings: in the Lord, neither men nor women can exist without the other.

What this passage shows us is that the distinction between the sexes is important to uphold within the new creation community because it supports the mutual dependence of one to another. God created humanity as male and female (Gen 1:26–28). Both are from God. Both are made in God's image. Both are charged to care for creation. Together, men and women form a full picture of humanity.

In 1 Cor 11:2–16, Paul's new creation teaching and his focus on reconciliation are further amplified through a very specific example of the relational dimension of mutual dependence between men and women. In Christ, the boundaries that separate men and women have been broken. By the indiscriminate outpouring of the Spirit, our ministry of reconciliation is made real in the midst of our mutual dependence on and submission to one another. Men and women are one in Christ. Yet Christ has taught us equality is not an end in itself, but exists for the sake of serving the other (Phil 2:5–11).

Bible Study and Discussion Questions

Read 1 Cor 11:1–16 and 12:1–31

1. 1 Cor 11:2–16 is a complicated and, at times, confusing biblical text. What stands out to you in the passage? What questions do you still have about the text's meaning?

2. Name the spiritual gifts in 12:8–10.

3. Where do these gifts come from, and what is their purpose (12:7)?

4. What is the difference between equality and sameness? Between diversity and discord?

5. Name the list of spiritual gifts in 12:28. Is the list hierarchical in order?

6. Do you think the lists (12:8–10 and 12:28) are meant to be exhaustive? Can you think of other spiritual gifts?

7. How does the metaphor of the body in 12:12–31 help Paul talk about:

   a. the unity of the believers?

   b. the variety of gifts within the church?

   c. the fallacy of spiritual pride and elitism?

For Reflection

1. Why do you think it is important to understand the issue of women's leadership in the church in light of what it means that Paul wants God's people to live as new creation, participating in the ministry of reconciliation with one another?

2. Where have you seen division along gender lines in the church? How do you think Paul's words in 1 Cor 11:11–12 apply to such situations?

Sojourner Truth: ca. 1797–1883

Born a slave in Ulster County, New York, Sojourner, who was named Isabella, was sold several times throughout her youth. When her last owner refused to follow New York law and set her free, she left on her own and stayed with an abolitionist family nearby. It was at this point in her life that she experienced her conversion, finding Jesus to be "altogether lovely,"[26] and became active in the local Methodist church. In 1843 Sojourner moved east, now

---

26. Quoted in Pope-Levison, *Turn the Pulpit Loose*, 51.

taking up her name, Sojourner, as she followed the Spirit's calling on her life. She worked as an evangelist at camp meetings, using her singing and preaching to testify to the "hope that was in her."[27] She also joined the Northampton Association for Education and Industry, a utopian community committed to transcending distinctions of gender, race, and class, which in turn led her to start speaking on the antislavery lecture circuit. She also connected with women's rights activists during her time in Northampton. She attended the Ohio Woman's Rights Convention in 1851 and gave her famous speech, "Ain't I a Woman?" During the Civil War, she focused her energy on providing necessary provisions for black soldiers and assisting freed slaves, even traveling to Kansas in 1879 to help a large group of freed Southern slaves get settled.

Testimony: The Reverend Susan Sytsma Bratt

Since 2010 the Reverend Susan Sytsma Bratt has served as the Associate Pastor at Northridge Presbyterian Church in Dallas, Texas. Prior to serving in Dallas she was a Lilly Resident Pastor at Bryn Mawr Presbyterian Church in Bryn Mawr, Pennsylvania for three years. A 2006 graduate of Princeton Theological Seminary, she was awarded the Jagow Prize in Homiletics & Speech and the Paul Reche Prize in Theology and Ministry. An alumna of Calvin College, with a BA in Religion, Susan was born and raised in Holland, Michigan and is married to Peter Bratt.

"What are you still doing in this denomination?" I was sitting across from a pastor who was interviewing me for an internship at a church outside Chicago that was in my denomination. This was one of my final steps in the ordination process after completing my master of divinity degree only a month before.

"I don't know anymore," I replied. I noted that my childhood congregation, where I was baptized and raised, was not supportive of women in ministry, and yet they had nurtured me. Digging deeper, I shared my grief and righteous indignation over the fact

27. Quoted in ibid., 52.

that we were still discussing women's ordination in 2006. I had already had to limit my options because not all churches were willing to take a female intern. Being male was still a requirement for ordination to be a minister of word and sacrament, and not many churches were willing to break the polity.

Yet as I continued reflecting on my journey I could not ignore that in spite of growing up in a congregation and denomination that did not affirm women's ordination, I had been profoundly nurtured. I was baptized, had made a profession of faith (confirmed), and had been commissioned on two youth summer mission trips. The elders at my home church invited me to stand in the pulpit and "share" about my experience. They loved and affirmed me. "You speak so well. You should do journalism." Ministers on those summer trips planted seeds. "Have you considered ministry?" they would ask. Professors at my alma mater and other mentors stood with me as I wrestled with the issue of my call and my gender.

I recalled that when it came time to attend seminary, instead of attending my denominational seminary, I broke rank and went to a seminary of a different denomination. How refreshing that was for me, not having to worry about proving myself or fighting to be heard. I had space to wrestle mightily with two calls: to the ministry of word and sacrament, and to my denomination and equality. I had decided to continue in the ordination process in my denomination, and to use my internship year to discern my next move. And then he asked that question.

He was right to ask me why I was sitting across from him. He could see that I no longer fit, that I did not have a place in my denomination anymore. He cut to the chase. Many women were waiting years to be called to serve a congregation. Several were ordained by exception to teach in schools or serve in the denominational ranks because there was no place for them anywhere else. He would be happy to mentor me.

At that watershed moment, it became clear to me: I could stay and wrestle and wait for the men of the denomination to advocate more strongly for women. Or, I could leave. Our denominational governing body, comprised of all male delegates, would discuss women's ordination yet again in 2007. That conversation had been going on for almost twenty years, and women still did not have a place at the table. I knew if I stayed I could not be patient and I would grow bitter.

And yet, these were my people. The denomination was a home for my maternal and paternal grandparents who immigrated from Germany and the Netherlands. The denomination cradled them, and helped them make their way in a strange land.

"They are not your people," my grandma would say to me as I contemplated denominational immigration. My own grandma knew the pain of saying goodbye, the grief of starting over, the sadness of living apart from those she held dear. She and my grandfather immigrated from Germany to Holland, Michigan in 1952. Yet, she chose to leave, to risk, and to start over in the United States at the age of twenty-five.

At the age of twenty-five, I too decided to pay the cost of passage and immigrate to a different denomination. I saw another land that contained opportunity and the promise for me to have full citizenship regardless of my gender.

Much like my immigrant grandparents who made a new home in North America, I have made a home among my new denomination. It is not the land of milk and honey. It is an imperfect denomination filled with imperfect people. Yet here I am able to minister and fully use my voice and the gifts God has given me.

My new denomination needs me, needs the gifts that my former denomination gave me: biblical literacy, theological depth, and confessional formation. I go back and visit the "old country" sometimes. I remember where I came from, what formed me, what carried me here to this new land where I have full citizenship.

For Reflection

1. Reflect on the challenges facing women called and gifted to leadership in the church if they have to navigate denominational barriers on the issue of women in ministry.

2. What stands out to you about the different experiences women might have from men on this issue of denominational navigation?

4

Remaining Biblical Issues & Women in Ministry

WHAT DOES GENESIS 1–3 INDICATE ABOUT THE RELATIONSHIP BETWEEN MEN, WOMEN, AND THE CURSE?

Genesis 1

As we already have seen in our investigation of 1 Corinthians 11 and as we will see, when we consider 1 Timothy 2, Genesis 1–3 are considered by Paul to be fairly crucial in his own understanding of male and female relations as set forth in Scripture. Indeed, as scholar Aída Besançon Spencer notes, "[a]lmost all foundational questions find their answer in the early chapters of Genesis."[1] Often, the church has operated with certain assumptions about men and women as having distinct, hierarchical roles which have been set forth from the time of creation and seen in the story of Adam and Eve in Genesis 1–3. For this reason, we must consider carefully the relation between Adam and Eve at creation and after the fall.

---

1. Spencer, *Beyond the Curse*, 17.

With this as our focus, we recognize first that Genesis 1 places a huge emphasis on humanity. Humanity is the last thing God created. All that God created was good, but when humankind was created God said it was "very good." Likewise, of all the things God created, humankind was the only thing made in God's image and likeness (1:26–27). The text uses a generic term for humankind (*'adam*) that means both "the human person" and "humanity" as well as "male and female." In other words, "'Adam' is a singular which represents the plural 'male and female.' By having the one 'Adam' represent the two 'male and female,' the writer has emphasized the essential unity and diversity of Adam and Eve."[2] Together, both are made in the image of God and both are given responsibility over creation. "Male and female share in power and authority, even as they share in dignity."[3] The responsibility comes to both, as a blessing, without any distinction of particular male or female responsibilities. They are to be fruitful, multiply, fill the earth, subdue it, and have dominion (1:28). In this opening chapter of Genesis, then, God sets out his good and perfect intention for humankind. Male and female were created together for partnership with one another and with God as part of God's plan to bless the whole world.

Bible Study and Discussion Questions

Read Genesis 1

1. What view of humankind does the text give us?

2. Define "dominion." With this in mind, talk about the way the text reveals the truth about this analogy: God is to humans as humans are to the creatures of the earth.[4]

3. Consider various ways the opening chapter of Genesis is important biblically and theologically.

2. Ibid., 21.

3. Ibid., 23.

4. Marshall, *A Guide through the Old Testament*, 25.

4. What is significant about the location of Genesis 1 within Scripture?

Genesis 2

Genesis 2 is a retelling of the creation story of Genesis 1. In this account, the human (*'adam*) is alone and in need of a companion. None of the other creatures God created qualify as a good partner (2:18–20). In fact, these creatures are named by the human in cooperation with God, putting them under the co-dominion of God and the human. God then makes a woman out of a part of the human (*'adam*). God differentiates the human (*'adam*) into man (*'ish*) and woman (*'ishshah*) in 2:21–22. The man and woman are equal persons who are differentiated from each other by their gender. This is indicated by the similar designations (*'ish/'ishshah*) and the same identification of bone and flesh (2:23). Some interpreters emphasize the fact that the man (*'adam*) says of the woman (*'ishshah*) that she is "bone of my bones" and "flesh of my flesh" and that she "shall be called woman" (2:23). They interpret this as an act of naming, thus signifying the authority of man over woman (like humanity's authority over and naming of the animals). However, the Hebrew word for "called" (2:23) is different from the act of naming (2:19–20). The man is not naming the woman. She was already designated "woman" when God differentiated *'adam* into *'ish* and *'ishshah* (2:21–22). Rather, the man sings about the wonder of what God has done to help him and acknowledges that God has given him an equal partner. The woman, as partner to the man, is not a *sub*ordinate helper. The word "helper" (*'ezer*) appears twenty-nine times in the Old Testament in reference to God—a *super*ordinate helper (i.e., Ex 18:4; Deut 33:7; Ps 27:9). Genesis 2 presents woman as a strong partner for man, which is why a man leaves his father and mother and cleaves to his wife (strong partner) and they become one flesh (2:24). Thus, just like Genesis 1, in Genesis 2 "Eve and Adam are equal in rank, equal in image.

Genesis 2, like Genesis 1, declares and explains male and female equality, joint rulership, and interrelationship."[5] The creation of male and female in Genesis 2, then, demonstrates again that male and female were created for equal partnership in the work God has for them to do—the creation of the woman was God's provision, in light of the man's insufficiency to care for the garden himself, of an equal helper able to share in the task of caring for the creation.

Bible Study and Discussion Questions

Read Gen 2:18–25; Ex 18:1–4; Deut 33:1, 7; Ps 27:9

1. What do you learn about God as helper in the following passages?

   • Ex 18:1–4

   • Deut 33:1, 7

   • Ps 27:9

2. Reflect on the similarity in the relationship between man and woman and that between God and humanity based on the repetition of the word "helper."

3. What is the significance of humanity's differentiation into male and female rather than remaining alone with only God as "helper"?

Genesis 3

Genesis 3 tells the story of sin's entrance into and disruption of God's good creation. The Hebrew text reveals that the woman and man sin together. The serpent addresses the woman in the plural "you" (3:1–5). In 3:6 the woman gives the fruit to her husband, who was with her. Both the man and the woman, who became one flesh again in 2:24, together disobeyed God. It is after this that

---

5. Ibid., 29.

judgment comes. Gen 3:14–19 is a description of what will become reality in the future. The effects of the curse are contrary to God's previous creation mandates for partnership. The new reality, under the curse, is that relationships have been tainted by sin and, for the first time, involve hierarchy. The supremacy/subjection relationship between the man and woman is not what God had in mind when he gave male and female equal dominion over the earth. It is in the story told in Genesis 3 that the entire created order gets out of whack. In many ways, the rest of Scripture is about reversing the effects of this chapter, culminating with God in Christ bringing life out of death and reconciling us back to God, one another, and creation. New creation comes through Christ's death on the cross. In Christ, the marred relationship between man and woman, a result of the fall, is restored to its original intent.

Bible Study and Discussion Questions

Read Gen 3:1–24

1. When faced with God's questions, what responses did the man and woman give?

2. How does the punishment of Adam and Eve differ? How is it the same?

3. What things are cursed by God in 3:14–19? Why are they cursed?

4. Why is it important to note that the sin of Adam and Eve destroyed their prior partnership?

Phoebe Palmer: 1807–1874

Phoebe Palmer was born in New York City into a family rich in piety. This greatly shaped her early social environment. Always religiously inclined, Phoebe knelt with her husband, Walter C. Palmer, at the Allen Street Methodist Church revival of 1832 and pledged her life to the promotion of holiness. In 1835, Phoebe and her sister established a women's prayer meeting that united two Methodist churches. Two years later, Phoebe testified to sanctifying grace in her life and soon became the leader of the prayer meeting. This became known as the Tuesday Meeting for the Promotion of Holiness. In 1839, men were allowed to attend the prayer meeting. Soon, Methodist bishops, theologians, and ministers were attending as well. This was the start of a renewal that would eventually impact all of American Methodism. In the 1840s, Phoebe and her husband began to travel around to churches, camp meetings, and conferences. Phoebe gave what she called "exhortations" and thus began her life of preaching. Her husband often set aside his medical practice to travel and assist Phoebe in her ministry. She played a big role in the holiness movement's expansion to national and international scope. Her influence was further increased by her writings and editing. She wrote articles for Methodist journals and books, such as *The Way of Holiness*, *Faith and Its Effects*, and *The Promise of the Father*. The Palmers also spent time ministering in the British Isles. After they returned to the states, they purchased *The Guide to Holiness*, a leading American journal about the Christian life. Phoebe became its editor from 1864 until her death. She was also active throughout her life in many missionary societies as well as welfare work.

What does Church Order and Pastoral Leadership Look Like in the Church and in Scripture?

Opposition to women's full participation in pastoral ministry often comes from churches that claim women are not to hold the positions of elder or head pastor. Some churches do not support the ordination of women to various pastoral or ministry positions. Church order in most churches today is not at all what it was in the early church, or in the churches to which Paul was writing his letters. Over the years, denominations have made decisions about how to label and structure various leadership positions within the church. There is nothing inherently wrong with this. However, Scripture never prescribes an exact form of church order to which faith communities must adhere. If anything, Paul's letters stress the importance of orderly worship, with leaders using their Spirit-given gifts and being people of good character.

What about the Pauline Specifications in 1 Timothy and Titus that a "Bishop" (Other Translations say "Overseer") is to be "the Husband of One Wife"?[6] Does that Mean Only Men can be Bishops?

Several things need to be said in response to these questions. The first is that Pauline lists are not designed to be "the standard" for all times and places. A cursory glance at 1 Timothy 3 and Titus 1 reveals differences in how the Pauline author shaped these similar lists—most likely to accommodate the recipients of the two letters. Even in Paul's day, the differences indicate that the lists were bound to a specific time and specific churches. This is not to say that the lists are to be disregarded today. Instead, they should be viewed as illustrative for the kinds of lists we are to create for our church leadership positions. Just as the Pauline author worked to remain relevant to the churches to whom the letters were sent by following the cultural norms of the day (i.e., the patriarchal context dictated that only men have positions of authority and leadership), so we need to come up with a new catalogue of church-leader qualifications that take into account the societal norms of our own day (i.e., equality between men and women, education, and experience).

Second, by looking into the Greco-Roman ethical teachings of Paul's day, it becomes clear that the qualities listed in 1 Timothy 3 and Titus 1 "reflect the virtues that were looked upon favorably by the Greco-Romans world."[7] These lists were very common, fairly

6. See 1 Tim 3:2, 12; Titus 1:6.
7. Bassler, *1 Timothy, 2 Timothy, Titus*, 63.

fixed in content, and supported a common ideal.[8] Additionally, the function of the lists in the letters are not to set out an office of the church but rather to outline the differences between those who qualify for church leadership positions and those who do not.[9]

Third, the Greek phrase "husband of one wife" had various definitions and connotations in that day, but when it is preceded by the adjective "blameless" (some translations say "above reproach"), like it is in 1 Tim 3:2 and Titus 1:6, "the most important point being made is that an overseer or supervisor ought to avoid any appearance of immorality."[10] In other words, it is not the gender of the leader that is being noted but rather their fidelity and integrity.

Finally, the term "bishop" in 1 Tim 3:16–17 and Titus 1:7 is the Greek word *episkopos*, meaning "overseer." This word is used "to refer to persons in positions of general oversight (especially in financial matters) as well as to specific officials of various civil and religious organizations."[11] New Testament scholar Luke Timothy Johnson translates *episkopos* as "supervisor" because of its very simple structure of leadership and lack of any Pauline theological legitimation. In view of this, these Pauline lists do not provide a basis for keeping women from important church leadership positions such as pastors, elders, and teachers.

What is the Nature of Pastoral Ministry and Ordination in the New Testament?

Ministry is based on gifts given to the people of God by the Spirit of God. The purpose of ministry is service to God and others. Authority in ministry derives from Christ, and all ministry ultimately resides in Christ who is "the apostle and high priest" (Heb 3:1), the "shepherd (pastor) and guardian (bishop) of our souls" (1 Pet 2:25), the "true teacher" (Matt 23:10; 1 John 2:27), the prophet

---

8. Ibid., 64.

9. Ibid., 65.

10. Johnson, *The First and Second Letters to Timothy*, 214.

11. Bassler, *1 Timothy, 2 Timothy, Titus*, 64.

and herald of the gospel (Luke 4:18; Acts 3:22), and the suffer-ing Servant (Luke 3:4–6; 4:17–19). Our ministry is performed by, through, in, and because of Jesus Christ. Furthermore, ministry is something in which the whole church participates. The work of the church is to equip all believers for ministry. God has called all believers to participate in a holy priesthood (1 Pet 2:5; Heb 13:15; Rev 1:6, 5:10). The New Testament indicates some people are given special forms of ministry, but, as we have seen, the distinction is never given according to gender, race, economic, or social status.

There are a few things to observe about what is called "or-dination" today. In New Testament times ordination involved the laying on of hands (1 Tim 4:14). It was also to release Paul to ministry (Acts 9:1–22). In Acts 6:1–6, it was a commissioning of some believers in order to free up the prophets and teachers to pursue their calling. Nowhere does the New Testament prescribe who should baptize, preside at the Lord's Supper, or lay on hands. Nor were these activities restricted to "apostles." In fact, the word "apostle" literally means "sent one." Again, it is in the giving of the Spirit that authority is given to men and women in order that they might use their Spirit-given gifts for all the people of God without restriction (1 Cor 12:4–11; Rom 12:4–8; Eph 4:11–13).

For Reflection

In your own words, describe what you think qualifies a person to serve in a position of leadership in church ministry.

Ida Robinson: 1891–1946

Ida was born in Hazelhurst, Georgia, the seventh of twelve chil-dren to Robert and Annie Bell. Having been converted as a teen-ager through an evangelistic street meeting, she began her own street evangelistic work in connection with The United Holy Church of America, becoming an ordained elder in 1919 and suc-cessfully serving as a pastor to a small mission church. Ida was displeased with the denomination's decreasing support for women in ministry, and, in 1924, following ten days of prayer and fasting, she began the process of starting a new denomination, The Mount Sinai Holy Church of America, believing that God was calling her "to loose the women."[12] The new denomination grew quickly along the eastern seaboard, and Ida served as both founder and leader over the whole denomination. She was a renowned preacher in both New York and Philadelphia, often preaching sermons that lasted several hours, and always emphasizing the doctrine of sanctification, calling people to repent from sin and live a holy life. The denomination had limitless opportunities for women to use their gifts for ministry. At the time of Ida's death in 1946, no less than "125 of the denomination's 163 ministers were women"[13] and there were eighty-four churches, a school in Philadelphia, a farm in South Jersey, and mission work in Cuba and Guyana.

How Are We to Understand Paul's Teaching on Submission in Eph 5:21–33?

In Ephesians, Paul is at pains to express the reality that while the power of sin has wrought division and strife within the entire cosmos, Christ's death, resurrection, and ascension have triumphed over sin and thereby created new life in Christ, peace, and unity. In light of the unity we have in Christ, Paul gives specific instructions on how the church is to live out this oneness (4:1—5:20). Flowing from these instructions for the church are Paul's specific admonishments to wives and husbands (5:21–33). "In other words, the church is not to depend upon the Christian home for its life, but rather the Christian home is to depend upon the church for its life. The quality of the family, and especially the relationship between husbands and wives, will mirror the quality of the congregation."[14] This is especially instructive as many in the church have been

12. Quoted in Pope-Levison, *Turn the Pulpit Loose*, 205.

13. Ibid., 208.

14. Williams, *The Apostle Paul and Women in the Church*, 89.

told the exact opposite—that the standard of female subordination to males begins in the home, in the relationship of wives to husbands, and is then carried forward into the church. Paul, however, wants familial relationships to be an extension of the new community relations established by the work of Christ. It is with this understanding in place that we find the opening verse (5:21) in Paul's section on wives and husbands functioning as a kind of topic sentence for the instructions that follow as well as serving as a connector to the instructions to the whole congregation that have come before it. Because all Christians have been made one in Christ, the new approach for all of our interactions is to be one of freely chosen mutual submission. From the new identity we have in Christ, husbands and wives are given specific ways to live out their mutual submission. Even though there is no explicit instruction for husbands to submit to their wives, the implication that they ought to is there not only in 5:21 but also in Paul's instructions about the way that husbands are to love their wives in 5:25, 28, and 33. The submission of wives to their husbands is discussed first (5:22–24), while Paul takes even more time to fill out what he desires for husbands in living out their submission to their wives (5:25–33). Wives and husbands are both given slightly different ways in which to live out their mutual submission to one another. Rather than this being an indicator of innate differences between the genders, it is more likely specific to the church context Paul is addressing. In other words, "the text is more likely addressing a problem women had with submission, that is, that they had trouble respecting their husbands, and a problem the husbands had with loving their wives. In each case, they need instruction because of their own lack not because of the nature of the other person."[15] When we consider that the common ancient patriarchal prescription for how households are to function did *not* center on sacrificial love but instead on male rulership and governance without consideration of love, the logic of Paul's approach stands out. He is calling for a rather distinct orientation of familial relationships

15. LaCelle-Peterson, *Liberating Tradition*, 110.

compared to the standards of the cultural world of the New Testament—one that is centered on the example of Christ.

Paul encourages women to subject themselves freely to the self-giving love of their husbands as an analogy to their submission to Christ. This idea of voluntary submission comes from the translation of the Greek word *hypotassomai* that Paul uses in 5:22. Paul is using the verb *hypotasso* ("subject to") in the middle voice, which in Greek is used to express "a voluntary action by the subject of the verb upon the subject of the verb."[16] Husbands are exhorted to express their mutual submission to their wives through self-sacrifice and self-giving love in the same manner of Christ's love for the church. In fact, Paul's instructions for the husbands to love (*agapao*) their wives (5:25) is also in the middle voice, which makes it almost identical to the instruction to the women (*hypotassomai*), in that both verbs in the middle voice express "giving up one's self-interest to serve and care for another's."[17]

The challenge in interpreting this passage has often centered around debates on how to understand Paul's use of the word "head" (*kephalē*) to describe both Christ and husbands (5:23). It is helpful to recall what we learned in our study of 1 Cor 11:2–16 about the meaning of *kephalē*: that the metaphor is one of origin not authority. Another helpful example where *kephalē* means "source" or "origin" is in Col 2:10. In that text, if *kephalē* had meant "authority," then Paul would be repeating the same idea three times, implying that Christ is the authority of all rule and authority instead of that Christ is the source of all rule and authority. Furthermore, when considering the whole passage of Eph 5:21–33 we see that Paul's imagery for Christ and the church is centered around the notion of Christ's headship as meaning that he takes care of his bride (the church) not that he lords it over her. Alan Padgett expresses it well: "Jesus takes the lead (*kephalē*) in being a servant, and his headship is not a role-hierarchy. This lord is also a servant, and this servant is also the Lord. Christians do indeed submit to Jesus, just as wives should submit to husbands; but Jesus has also submitted to us in

16. Bristow, *What Paul Really Said*, 40.
17. Ibid., 42.

love and taken up the role of a slave for us in the economy of salvation history. Husbands should do likewise in relation to their
wives. Free, loving, and mutual submission is the way of following
after Jesus in true discipleship."[18] Following Paul, then, we see that
the meaning of both leadership (headship) and submission derives
from the person and work of Jesus Christ, especially in consideration of the marriage analogy being drawn in this passage between
Christ and his bride, the church. To lead for Paul is to be a servant,
it is not to lord authority over others. In this way, we see that the
instructions to husbands and wives in this passage, although different, are both centered on self-giving and mutual submission.
Indeed, 5:21 is the summary for all the parts that make up Eph
5:21–33.

What Are We To Make of the Church's Interpretation of 1 Tim 2:9–15, which Prevents Women's Leadership in the Church?

The church has affirmed the role of Scripture in shaping all aspects
of the life and work of the individual believer and church universal. For this reason, the interpretation of key biblical texts (such as
1 Tim 2:9–15; 1 Cor 11:2–16; Eph 5:21–33; etc.) directly correlates
with women's freedom or restriction to participate fully in church
leadership. Whether or not interpretation shapes reality or reality dictates interpretation is a hard question to answer. Although
women are seen as leaders throughout all of Scripture, overwhelm-
ingly it is the instructions and portraits from the Pauline letters
of the New Testament that have been the most influential in the
history of the church and interpretation on this issue.

Without a doubt, if there was one text in the Bible that has
been used more than any other to prevent women from full participation in church ministry it has been 1 Tim 2:9–15. For centuries
Christians have been caught between the seeming contradiction
between 1 Tim 2:9–15 compared to other biblical texts and the

18. Padgett, *As Christ Submits to the Church*, 67.

testimony of women throughout history who have been used powerfully by God and yet seem to defy the teaching of 1 Timothy 2. The writings of the early church fathers and great reformers show a fairly consistent "traditional" or "historical" interpretation of this Pauline text. This interpretation has said that women are forbidden to teach and make decisions over men. Some scholars have maintained that the reason for such a prohibition is that women, like Eve, are easily deceived. They should not teach or lead because they are apt to lead people astray.

Throughout the twentieth century many conservative scholars have assumed the traditional interpretation of 1 Timothy 2, although they have diverged from the "historic" interpretation in a few ways. For example, conservative scholars today emphasize that the need for such restrictions on women should only occur in the church and at home instead of in all arenas of life as previously taught by the church fathers and reformers.[19]

A conservative interpretation has not been the only voice on this text, though. Mary Slessor, the great Scottish missionary of Calabar, once wrote in her Bible beside this text, "'Nay, Paul laddie! This will na' do.'"[20] Many women evangelists of the late eighteenth and early nineteenth century dealt with the passage in light of Acts 2, the portrait of Priscilla in Acts 18, and other more positive references to women in Paul's letters. More recently, this text has been scrutinized under the lens of the historical critical method of biblical examination. Many scholars since the 1960s have paid more attention to the social world of Paul's day, as well as to the rhetorical and theological motifs of 1 Timothy, in order to give a clearer picture of how this passage addresses particular women or circumstances and, therefore, how the text cannot be taken out of context and applied universally in the church today.

19. Giles, "A Critique of the 'Novel,'" 202.
20. Quoted in Kroeger and Kroeger, *I Suffer Not a Woman*, 13–14.

Bible Study and Discussion Questions

Read 1 Timothy 1–2 two times

1. Paul states his reason for writing to Timothy. What is that reason?

2. Prayer seems to be a key word in 1 Timothy 2. Write down the verses that use various synonyms for "prayer," such as the words "entreaties," "prayers," "petitions," "thanksgivings," and "pray."

3. Make a list of what you learn about prayer from this chapter. Answer *who, what, when, where, why,* and *how* questions regarding prayer. For example, who is told to pray? What are they to pray about?

4. Write down references to God and Jesus Christ, including those references to God or Jesus Christ using the pronouns "he," "him," and "his." List what you learn about each reference.

5. Read 1 Tim 2:9–15 again. Keeping in mind Paul's stated reason for writing his letter to Timothy, answer the following questions:

   a. What is Paul saying specifically about women?

   b. Where is Paul teaching that this behavior be practiced or not be practiced?

   c. What are Paul's reasons for his instructions?

   d. Is this appropriate to our culture today?

   e. If it is not appropriate to our culture, why not?

   f. If it is, how should this be practiced today?

   g. Are there other biblical texts that have anything to say about this passage, one way or the other?

How Do We Understand the Meaning of 1
 2:9–15 and Apply it Today?[21]

As noted already, when we come to this particular passage we must do so in a way that realistically acknowledges the way this biblical text has been misused throughout the history of the church to silence women and to prevent them not only from speaking and leading in church settings but also from using their God-given gifts to lead and teach in other areas of life. At the same time, it is important to remember that this text has value and import for Christians just like any other biblical text. The challenge is to hear this passage in its own context and then to do the important work of interpretation by which we carefully seek after its application to our life in Christian community today. Neither do we want to hinder this passage in its capacity as revelatory text nor do we want to read more into this passage than what is appropriate considering its specific cultural location and instructions to one particular community.

While this text contains a set of Pauline instructions for women within the worship setting that follows in the footsteps of well-known patterns of ancient feminine ideals (i.e., Paul is not reinventing the wheel in his request for women to demonstrate their upstanding nature through their dress [2:9], works of mercy [2:10], and attention to education [2:11–12]), what we must concern ourselves with is to consider the theological motivations that prompted Paul to reiterate these common ideals for middle class women in the Greco-Roman world of his day. Here is where our careful reading of 1 Timothy 2 (not to mention the rest of the letter and 2 Timothy as well) comes into play. In 2:1–7 we learn that the reason Paul wants the community to pray for all people

21. My interpretation of this text is heavily influenced by the work of Robert W. Wall, most especially his essay "1 Timothy 2:9–15 Reconsidered (Again!)," his commentary *1 & 2 Timothy and Titus*, and his address at a forum on this subject on February 27, 2003 at Seattle Pacific University. I am personally grateful to him for his concern and care with this passage, which was of tremendous help to me during my days as a student as I wrestled deeply with this passage and its history of interpretation.

is because he is firmly convinced that his apostolic mission flows from the truth of the one God, who desires the salvation of all people, and the one mediator, Jesus Christ, who gave of himself in order to purchase the salvation of all people. Paul directly connects the mission of the church to the mission of the triune God. This connection of the church's mission in the world to the mission of the triune God is carried forward into his specific instructions to men (2:8) and women (2:9–15) by the use of "therefore" (2:8) and "likewise" (2:9a). "Paul's purpose is simply this: the congregation's worship practices, down to the individual believer, should personify the redemptive purpose of God our Savior set out by the preceding theological formulation"[22] in 2:1–7.

In the interest of cutting to the chase, let us first focus our attention on 2:11–15a. In the history of this text's misuse, 2:12 is often isolated from the rest of the passage. It is important to re-attach 2:12 to 2:11. When the two verses are read together, what we see is that the key emphasis is on Paul's command that a woman learn. Further, he focuses on the way in which a woman is to learn. He notes that she should learn "with quietness." The Greek word used is *hēsychia*. This is a word that describes an appropriate way to learn. The same word is used to described the whole community in 2:2b, not to mention its use as a descriptor for men in Acts 22:2; 1 Thess 4:11; 2 Thess 3:12; and 1 Pet 3:4.[23] Thus, if Paul had wanted to keep women from speaking, we might expect to see him use the word *epistomizō*, rather than *hēsychia*. In Titus 1:11, Paul uses *epistomizō* when he tells Titus to silence some of the Jewish Christians whose vocal arguments were causing great disruptions within the church.[24] In contrast, *hēsychia* means that one is astutely attentive to what is going on around oneself. In addition to asking that a woman learn in this manner, Paul also qualifies her learning with another imperative, "to submit." In this context, it is best to understand a woman's submission to what is taught in order that

22. Wall, *1 & 2 Timothy and Titus*, 87.

23. Oden, *First and Second Timothy and Titus*, 96.

24. Wall, *1 & 2 Timothy and Titus*, 90n39.

she might learn. This word also underscores the emphasis Paul puts on the attitude of heart that is to accompany learning.

To whom must a faithful woman submit in order to learn? What teaching must she heed in order to learn? The answer comes in 2:12. If a woman is to learn, she cannot teach at the same time. She must submit to the instruction and authority of a good male teacher. The patriarchal context of Ephesus (not to mention the culture of Judaism in that day), where Timothy is organizing a new congregation, dictates that the role of teacher is open only to well-trained men. First Timothy 2:12 mentions both teaching and having authority. To connect these two ideas, like Paul does, means that to teach is to exercise authority over another. Wall notes that "*authentein* principally refers to virtuous teachers who are 'apt to teach' (cf. 3:2). Second, the apostle recognizes a special familial relationship with his delegated successors [most especially here is Timothy], whose spiritual birthright as his 'children' . . . gives them special authority to teach others."[25] Therefore, while Paul's instructions in 2:12 specify that a woman is not to teach or have authority over a man (*anēr*), this does not mean that Paul is here defining "the authority of a teacher in gender-specific terms but rather in terms of charisma or in a manner consistent with the content and redemptive consequence of his gospel."[26]

Having re-attached 2:11 and 2:12, they must together be re-attached to 2:9-15. First Timothy 2:11-12 is part of Paul's larger instructions for Christian women that begin in 2:9. Like the repetition of the phrase "with quietness" in 2:11-12, Paul uses the phrase "with modesty" (or "prudence," *sophrosynē*) in 2:9 and 2:15. Paul's emphasis on modesty, like his assumption that teachers are male, again comes from the cultural mores of his day. Popular philosophers taught that the ideal woman was characterized by the virtue of modesty. This represented both her maturity and religious

25. Ibid., 92.

26. Ibid. Wall points to 1 Timothy's repeated use of the *didaskein* family of words (see 1:10; 4:6, 11, 13, 16; 5:17; 6:1, 2; cf. 1:3; 6:3) as demonstrating both the correct manner of Pauline catechesis as well as distinguishing between authorized teachers and those who must be taught and corrected for their *heterodidaskalein*, "divergent teaching" (see 1:3-4, 20). Ibid., 92-93.

commitment. Paul reflects this philosophy in 2:9–10. Again, recall that Paul's instructions are grounded in the theological idea that a congregation must worship God in a manner that reflects God's desire to save everyone. First Timothy 2:4–6 states that the vocation of the community of worship is to assist with God's desire that all people be saved. While Paul gives different instructions regarding worship and church practice to various churches in order to allow for the various cultural conventions in the different places, he does not change his belief that God wants to save everyone.

It is this overarching theological theme in 1 Timothy 2 that helps us to see the connection between 2:11–12 and the commentary Paul gives on Eve's story in 2:13–15a. In the past, commentators have looked at these verses on Eve as Paul's reason for restricting Christian women from teaching or having authority over men. They have argued that Eve set a precedent for all women as weak-minded and easily deceived. This interpretation directly contradicts Paul's teaching that in Christ Jesus we are freed for a new life (see Rom 5:12—6:23). In fact, according to Paul's theology, this would be to deny the liberation from such evils accomplished by God's grace through Jesus' death and resurrection and subsequent empowerment by the Spirit. Eve's story in Genesis chapters 2–4, when seen in light of the theological subtext of 1 Timothy 2, highlights Paul's belief that everyone's conduct in the church facilitates God's saving grace.

First Timothy 2:13–15a highlights the story of Eve from the beginning, middle, and end. First Timothy 2:13 is Eve's creation from Adam (Gen 2:21–23). First Timothy 2:14 is the climax of Eve's deception and sin (Gen 3:1–13), and 2:15a is Eve's redemption and new life (Gen 4:1–2). The reference to salvation through childbearing is metaphorical. If it were literal, Paul would be denying that sinners are saved through Jesus alone, limiting salvation only to women who give birth to children. Paul's commentary on Eve's story indicates that God saves women as women. As the story in Genesis 4 begins, Eve, upon giving birth to her first child, discovers that her relationship with God is still intact and celebrates her partnership with God in giving life to another. In other words, the reference to Eve's childbearing in 1 Tim 2:15a does not point back to the judgment she receives in Gen 3:16 but to her exclamation in Gen 4:1b of having made a person with God, "a note that sounds her post-Eden reconciliation with God. In evident absence of the earlier prediction of increased pain, the woman realizes that God has chosen her to fulfill the creational promise of Gen 1:28. . . . Paul's use of Eve's story, then, is typological of every woman who when giving birth to a new life—a uniquely female experience—is awakened to a realization of her partnership with God, who has not abandoned her because of Christ Jesus."[27]

In conclusion, we have seen that Paul's main point in 2:11–12 is that women are to learn quietly. The Christian woman is to be attentive to what she is taught. Paul is not trying to hold back a group of liberated Christian women. He is merely providing guidelines for their religious training in a manner in line with the religious training offered in that part of the ancient world. He is asking Christian women to learn attentively only from those men who are authorized because of their own training and spiritual maturity. A Christian woman is not to learn from just any man. Not all teachers have been teaching healthy Christian doctrine. Christian women who learn attentively from qualified teachers reflect their modesty and are well respected in both church and society. In Paul's world, if Christian men were violent and Christian women dressed indecently and failed to learn properly, they would be considered shameful by the surrounding culture and the gospel that they proclaim would be discredited.

Finally, what does the act of childbearing teach about God's salvation? First of all, only women can bear children. Paul, radically deviating from the philosophy of his day, teaches that God's purpose is to save women as women. Eve, as representative of all women, is not only differentiated from Adam by her ability to give birth to children, but also spiritually. The salvation of a woman as a woman stays in line with her creation as female by God. This point is illustrated in Gen 4:1. Eve gives birth to her first child and comments that she has partnered with God to make a man. She

---

27. Ibid., 96–97.

does not say that she made a man with Adam. Her partnership with God in Genesis 4 is important because it happens after she has sinned, been deceived, and kicked out of the Garden with Adam. The theological theme of her joy in giving birth is that this experience of childbearing—a distinctively female experience—reminds her that she is not separated from God after all. God still loves her and wants to partner with her, something promised to both the man and the woman in Genesis 1. Paul uses the image of childbearing as a metaphor of a unique female experience of new life with the God who forgives. Therefore, the social manners of a Christian woman, exhibited through modesty in public life and worship and in the manner of her learning, are in line with the church's call to live out the gospel in a way that attracts non-believing women to God.

Bearing all of this in mind, the only thing left to do in recovering a faithful reading and application of 1 Tim 2:9–15 is to re-attach it to the rest of the New Testament. To do this is to recall to mind other biblical texts that come before 1 Timothy 2 such as John 4; Acts 2 and 18; 1 Cor 11–12; and Gal 3:28. These texts serve to relativize Paul's instructions to Timothy. First Timothy 2:9–15 cannot trump all other Scripture when defining the role of a woman in church ministry. However, the theological theme present in 1 Timothy 2 should always regulate how Christians think about gender and Christian ministry today. In other words, God desires to save all people. Moreover, a Christian's vocation has an important role to play in God's work to save sinners from death. In our culture today, to prevent competent, mature Christian women from the teaching office of the church (or full participation in church ministry) will only hinder the spread of the gospel that Paul is so concerned about in 1 Timothy.

Amanda Berry Smith: 1837–1915

Born in Maryland and the oldest girl in a family of thirteen children to slaves Samuel and Mariam Berry, Amanda struggled to get educated as a child. Most of her education occurred at home until she moved away to work as a live-in domestic. She became active in a Methodist church, but was forced by her class leader to be taught last, which made her late to work and so she quit attending in order to keep her job. In 1855, Amanda became seriously ill and had a dream that she was preaching at a camp meeting. She was soon converted and received a divine call to preach. She responded by attending camp meetings, sharing her gifts of singing and preaching with as many as 8,000 people at a time. She also preached in other countries, such as India, Great Britain, and West Africa, where she also adopted two children. Later in life she founded the Amanda Smith Orphanage and Industrial Home for Abandoned and Destitute Colored Children in Harvey, Illinois, but she was never able to get enough funding to improve the school's living conditions, which were subpar. Throughout her life Amanda experienced firsthand the challenge of fitting in due to her race and gender, even being accused by some African Americans of "abandoning her race to cater to whites,"[28] yet ultimately expressing contentment over her color, remarking that "'God's choice is the best and most substantial.'"[29]

Testimony: The Reverend Traci Smith

The Reverend Traci Smith is pastor of Northwood Presbyterian Church in San Antonio and author of Seamless Faith: Simple Practices for Daily Family Life *(2014), a book that helps families make meaningful connections together through tradition, ceremony, and spiritual practice. To connect with Traci, visit www.traci-smith.com.*

The Daughters of Zelophehad

The question often comes amid long car rides, or youth trips, or awkward social mixers: "If you could have a conversation with anyone, dead or alive, who would it be?" I always answer, "One of

28. Pope-Levison, *Turn the Pulpit Loose*, 92.
29. Quoted in ibid., 93.

the daughters of Zelophehad," to which the predictable follow up question is, "Who?" I give this answer in order to share the story from Numbers 27 and 36. In that story, a man named Zelophehad dies, and his five daughters, Mahlah, Noah, Hoglah, Milcah, and Tirzah, are left with no right to inherit their father's land because they are women. They plead their case to Moses, asking why should the name of their father be taken away from his clan because he had no son. The sisters then demand Moses give them a possession among their father's brothers. Moses hears their request and takes it to God, and God sides with the daughters. Later, their decision is appealed and amended to restrict whom they can marry, but then it is ultimately upheld.

When I happened upon this story a few years ago, it felt like something that was uniquely mine. Not only did I find it on my own, divorced from the often ugly and arduous sermon writing process, but I found it at a time when I was unsure of my place in the male-dominated world of pastoring. This story is about women standing up, asking for something that rightfully belongs to them, and receiving it. For me, it did not take fancy hermeneutics, word studies, or a preaching angle to be inspired. It was just a straight-forward story about brave women who took a stand.

I am a female solo pastor, not yet thirty-five, and much of my congregation have daughters my age. And so when I (young, female, never-done-this-before Traci) take risks and chart new paths, it is easy to feel self-conscious and alone. When I feel like I am going against culture or standing up for something that should be mine already, Mahlah, Hoglah, Noah, Milcah, and Tirzah are there in the background, whispering in my ear, "We understand. We did it, too." They remind me that the need for women to stand up and ask for what is rightfully theirs is not new. Women have been fighting this fight for hundreds upon thousands of years.

Though the sisters are long gone, their story is very real to me. If we had the chance to have a conversation, I know just what I would ask them, and maybe the mystery of resurrection will allow that some day. In the meantime, I settle for face-to-face conversations with other trailblazing women.

The story of Zelophehad's daughters is so moving precisely because the daughters are not lumped together, we learn all five names: Noah, Hoglah, Milcah, Tirzah, and Mahlah. In that spirit, I am moved to mention other women who are also there when I need a role model by name (or, for confidentiality, by initial). These women, like my favorite biblical sisters, are not my peers. They blazed these trails long ago. I think of Ms. B, a member of my congregation and a retired university professor. She told me the story of how she decided to go back to college after her children were in grade school and said, "I loved it so much I decided to go straight through for a PhD." Then there's octogenarian Ms. J, who told me about how she started her internationally successful herb business with one tiny crop of herbs growing in a whisky barrel. I want to name Ms. H, who leaned in to my ear from her wheelchair and said, "I liked you before I even met you. I figure any woman brave enough to take a man's job is a friend of mine." Ms. H's neighbor in the retirement home had the opposite, but equally affirming reaction on the same day when she said, "At first I wasn't sure about you. A woman pastor? But then I listened to you, and you can preach."

These women cheer me on, and propel me forward. I listen to their voices when other voices say, in roundabout, or sometimes overt ways, "Why should I take direction from you? You're young. You're female. You know nothing." Stories of others who have been there first are critically important, not just for me, but for other women who aim to lead. These stories need to be heard. Notably, the story of the daughters of Zelophehad is not in the Revised Common Lectionary. A faithful churchgoer could attend church every week for three years and, even if that church read each and every lectionary text assigned for the week, that churchgoer would never hear their story. This fact made me reconsider the merits of preaching the lectionary exclusively, and now I sometimes use the lectionary and put it aside other times.

But the story of Zelophehad's daughters did not just change the way I preach, it changed the way I think. When I read the many blog posts, articles, and books that talk about how women "nowadays" struggle to balance home and work life or how women are "beginning" to speak truth to power, I remember my sisters, Mahlah, Noah, Hoglah, Milcah, and Tirzah. I remember that their story, passed by though it may be, is my story. I will forever be grateful to them for that gift.

For Reflection

1. If you are unfamiliar with it, read the story of the daughters of Zelophehad in Num 27:1–11 and 36:1–12. Why might it be important for women leaders in the church to have biblical and other, more current, role models who are women?

2. Why might it be important for men today to have and know both biblical and current-day women leaders in the church?

5

Church History & Women in Ministry

Why is it Important to Look at Women in Ministry in the History of the Church?

In the introduction to *Her Story: Women in Christian Tradition*, Barbara J. MacHaffie suggests a careful collection of historical data along with well-defined principles for its reinterpretation will provide a "usable past for women" that will help "dispel stereotypes, illumine current issues in the Christian community, and build up the sense of self-worth of women."[1] MacHaffie's point is that investigation into the church's history in relationship to women in ministry by considering the forces that have shaped the church's present and sincerely investigating beyond the bounds of the story as we have been told gives us a perspective today we would not otherwise have access to. Reinterpretation of the historical data regarding women in the church brings to light the stories of countless women who have had experiences in the church, good and bad, made contributions in ministry, recognized or not, and manifested spiritual power for the benefit of others, both inside and outside of traditional positions of authority. For those who might mistakenly believe that women are only now beginning to voice their displeasure at being held back from various church offices or

1. MacHaffie, *Her Story*, 3.

ministry positions, a brief review of women's actual participation and leadership in the life of the church is helpful in dispelling the notion that women were once passive recipients of the limitations imposed on them by men. As LaCelle-Peterson rightly points out, you do not "have to keep saying 'Be quiet' if no one is making noise."[2] The reality is that many faithful Christian women are to be thanked, remembered, and honored for the invaluable part they played in bringing the Christian church to where it is today. Unfortunately, because women have far too often gone unnamed, forgotten, or dismissed, many today suffer under the illusion that the story so often told by Christian tradition, that women were not vitally at work in each stage of the church's history, is actually true.

For Reflection

Before moving on, pause for a moment and consider what you know about the story of women leaders in the history of the church. If you can, list any names of women and describe briefly their leadership roles.

Aimee Semple McPherson: 1890–1944

Aimee Semple McPherson was a well-known evangelist whose ministry was based in Southern California from the 1920s through the 1940s. Her church, Angelus Temple, located in the Los Angeles area, became widely known because of her dramatic and well-presented sermons. At its height, Angelus Temple had more than 5,300 people attending each service. Aimee would literally preach to tens of thousands of people every week. Another facet of Angelus Temple's ministry was providing food and job assistance to scores of people struggling through the economic hardships of the time period. In the early 1920s, Aimee established the International Church of the Foursquare Gospel. The Foursquare denomination continues to this day.

2. LaCelle-Peterson, *Liberating Tradition*, 152.

WHAT LEADERSHIP POSITIONS HAVE WOMEN HAD THROUGHOUT CHURCH HISTORY?

This is a question that requires a much more thorough answer than we can give it here. For the sake of brevity, we will pause only to consider the contributions and leadership of women in the church throughout three main earlier eras of the church: the early church, the medieval church, and the Reformation church. Because we have devoted seven out of our twelve biographical sketches to women leaders throughout the history of the church in America, we will bypass that portion of the church's history. The goal of this section is to demonstrate just how many roles and contributions women made and continue to make to the church throughout its existence.

For Reflection

Take a few minutes to review the biographical sketches of the seven women leaders in the church in America[3] and then, from those sketches, write a brief paragraph that describes the various roles of women leaders in the church throughout America's history.

Women in the Early Church[4]

As a result of the many surviving early church documents restricting women's involvement, scholars often have assumed that only men were leaders in the early church, but there is now a growing body of evidence suggesting that, from the very beginning, women were involved in all aspects and levels of church ministry, including, but not limited to, the ordained positions of deacon, priest, and bishop. One example is Bishop Theodora, who was one of four female saints rendered in a mosaic in a Roman basilica. There is

3. See pages 47–48, 56–57, 60–61, 72–73, 78–79, 83, and 86.

4. Used in this section: LaCelle-Peterson, *Liberating Tradition;* and Torjesen, *When Women Were Priests.*

also now evidence indicating that many women were given the title of apostle or evangelist as a result of their preaching ministries. In addition to Junia, who we have already discussed, there were others such as Thecla, one of Paul's ministry partners who preached and performed baptisms, and Nino, who is credited with converting the royal family in Georgia and was ordained to the ministry of preaching Christ's divinity and resurrection wherever the Spirit led her.

Women were also influential theology teachers both in monastic settings as well as in church worship. Proba, a theological teacher from the third century, wrote the *Cento*, which made use of lines from Virgil to retell biblical stories and was used for hundreds of years to teach the Bible to people. Melania the Younger and Macrina were both teachers of theology; the former taught the Bible to men and women, the latter, in addition to her expositions on Christian Scripture, was also well known for her theological, philosophical, and scientific teaching.

Some of the more recent historical scholarship has focused on inscriptions, letters, and other literary documents that designate women as presbyters, or priests, well into the eighth century. The reality, however, of women priests is that there was always controversy surrounding their sacramental roles. Different times in the history of the church represent changes to what was considered acceptable practice. In reality, the relationship of the church to the empire as well as the increasingly male-dominated culture often worked more strongly against women's participation than any hard scriptural arguments.

In the East, both men and women were ordained to the office of deacon and had duties that included assisting bishops, anointing and teaching those baptized into the faith, bringing communion to those unable to come to church, and caring for the poor and the sick. The Christian historian Eusebius recorded information about women prophets, including Ammia of Philadelphia, without feeling the need to mention their sex. During the third century, the role of prophets merged into that of martyr and confessor, of which there were just as many women as men. As martyrs, women could publicly testify to their faith, be officially recognized as church heroes worth emulating, and have their story live on in devotional literature and special feast days.

Discussion Questions

1. Do an internet search of women martyrs in the early church.

2. List the names of women martyrs you find documented.

3. Pick one of the names and do a little more research into the story of that woman's martyrdom. Describe briefly what you learned about her story.

Women in the Medieval Church[5]

Despite the writing of medieval theologians, such as Thomas Aquinas, who argued that women were subordinate to men in the created order and intellectually and morally inferior, the supposed Dark Ages was initially a time when Christian women were coming into their own, often playing an indispensable part in the survival and growth of the church. One prime example is the role played by three Christian princesses: Clotilde, Bertha, and Ethelburga, who each were responsible for converting their pagan husbands to Christianity and thus were strong forces behind the spread of Christianity to parts of France and England.

At the same time, images of women from this era were caught between two extremes: either they were denounced as being wicked and inferior or they were idealized in the symbol of the Virgin Mary. As a result, virginity was often seen as the best lifestyle for women and came at the expense of women having to reject their sexuality and femininity. Even so, this particular ascetic lifestyle also provided women with the benefits of freedom, protection, travel, power, and sometimes leadership and authority.

---

5. Used in this section: MacHaffie, *Her Story;* and Malone, *Women and Christianity.*

Moreover, there were several different ways the lifestyle could be achieved and maintained by women: through domestic asceticism, in monastic communities, and within a spiritual marriage. One of the few existing spiritual biographies from this time period was one written by Margery Kempe, who, as a result of some dramatic spiritual experiences, persuaded her husband to participate with her in a celibate marriage, after having fourteen children. Kempe was always regarded by male clergy with suspicion because she believed she had equal right to teach and advise others as a result of her spiritual experiences.

One leadership role women held in the church during this time was that of abbess, the head of a monastery for women. Some abbesses, such as Hilda of Whitby, Tetta of Wimborne, and Frideswide of Oxford, presided over what were known as "double" monasteries for both men and women. One abbess, Hugerberc of Hildesheim, wrote *Hodoeporicon*, which is not only the sole piece of writing we have from any abbess but also one of the first German language travelogues, notably emphasizing the missionary role women played in the evangelization of Germany.

Not only were abbesses entrusted with the spiritual and institutional leadership of such Christian communities, they often had the same kind of power and privileges as male abbots, bishops, and noblemen. While abbesses were not permitted to administer the sacraments, they did give spiritual counsel, hear confessions, administer penance, and grant absolution for sins. Unfortunately, this "high" role for women did not continue unabated but instead declined in the later Middle Ages as a result of the writings of Protestant Reformers and the patriarchal culture of the Renaissance period. As the church became more and more of a male club, women were blamed for every bad thing that befell them, being viewed as troubled creatures, unable to survive without the oversight of men and better off enclosed in a patriarchal marriage or cloistered away, out of sight, often into highly structured Benedictine monasteries. Monasticism, unfortunately, started to shed any trace of equality and partnership between the sexes and became highly clericalized.

Discussion Questions

1. Pick one of the Christian princesses to research on the internet. Give a brief summary of her story and role.

2. Pick one of the abbesses to research on the internet. Write a summary of her story and contribution to the church.

Henrietta Mears: 1890–1963

Henrietta is known as a woman of great vision. Billy Graham once remarked that he doubts "if any other woman outside of my wife and mother has had such a marked influence [on my life]. She is certainly one of the greatest Christians I have ever known!"[6] In 1928 Henrietta became the director of Christian education at the First Presbyterian Church in Hollywood, California. After her arrival, Sunday school attendance at the church skyrocketed from four hundred to four thousand. During her time at First Presbyterian, more than four hundred young people entered full-time Christian service. Henrietta noticed that Sunday school literature left much to be desired, and so she began writing her own lessons. It was not long before churches all over the country began requesting copies of her material. When the demand became too great, she established Gospel Light Publications, one of the first publishers in the field of Christian education.

Women in the Reformation Church[7]

The Reformation era was a time of enormous change in the church and, subsequently, for the role and place of women. Where once women had been confined to monasteries, even against their will, and celibacy was the ideal, now the institution of marriage was seen in a more positive light, allowing women to have a role in the

6. Quoted in Wilke, "Gospel Light."

7. Used in this section: LaCelle-Peterson, *Liberating Tradition;* and Marshall, *Women in Reformation and Counter-Reformation Europe.*

home as directors of the spiritual formation of their children. Even so, many women suffered a tremendous loss of freedom with the closing of so many convents and their options for acceptable religious work outside of the home all but disappeared. While former priests and monks could find new roles serving as a pastor, former nuns had no ministerial options. The Protestant teaching of the priesthood of all believers inspired women as well as men, yet the women who tried to live into that by practicing the ministry of preaching were condemned and often banished from their cities.

Overall, there is a great disparity between the insights we can gain about women's roles from the theological writings of men and other historical sources and the ability they had to form their own religious identity apart from men. For example, Luther and Calvin both explicitly reject the notion of women preachers in their writings. On the other hand, we have a published tract written by a noblewoman, Ursula of Munsterberg, in which she corrects the false impressions her family had about her decision to leave the convent and clearly articulates her own Protestant sensibilities and identity to them. In general, we can say that women were both enslaved and liberated during this time in church history. Inasmuch as domesticity was the overarching model women were forced to live within, they were incredibly confined. However, for women who were able, in various ways, to circumvent or reinvent this restrictive model, there were some avenues for independence, public activity, and recognition.

One public avenue for proclaiming the faith that still persisted for women was that of martyrdom. In this time period, the female martyrs in Germany were Anabaptists, including one known as Claesken, who upset the authorities because of her powerful ability to convert many people. Records of their interrogations indicate that these Anabaptist women were outstanding in their articulation of theological doctrine and biblical passages. For women married to Protestant pastors, there were opportunities to practice the ministry of hospitality to the many students and refugees who spent time in their home and often to contribute to theological discussions that took place there. Luther's wife, Katherine von Bora, and the highly educated wife of Urbanus Rhegius, are two such examples of Reformer's wives who participated in the theological discussions of their households. Rhegius published the discussions between himself and his wife because he believed they were valuable teaching tools for disseminating Lutheran ideas.

In a more dramatic fashion, Isabella of Castile was a Spanish social, religious, and political reformer intent on creating unity and independence for her country. In England, Anne Askew was an early Protestant believer who sought, but was not granted, a divorce from her Catholic husband due to their religious differences. She joined up with a group of Reformers in London who were connected with Queen Catherine Parr, eventually being arrested for her views on the Mass, tortured in the Tower of London for heretical preaching, and, in an attempt to learn the names of those in her group, executed by fire at the age of twenty-five. In Hungary, three noblewomen—Mary, wife of King Louis II; Isabella, wife of John Zápolya; and Elizabeth Nádasdy, who was known as the Blood Countess—are each impressive for their relative independence and influence on the spread of the Reformation in their country, even as their gender meant they were always constrained within the limits of familial responsibilities.

Discussion Questions

1. Pick one of the Hungarian noblewomen to research on the internet. Give a brief summary of her story and role in the spread of the Reformation in Hungary.

2. How would you characterize the similarities and differences for women in ministry across the three eras of church history?

Dorothy Day: 1897–1980

Dorothy Day grew up in a poor working-class neighborhood. As a young girl, she was playing in the attic with her sister when she came across a Bible and began reading it. She later remembered that this discovery had a profound effect on her life. An avid reader, she went to college when she was just sixteen years old. Later, as a nurse, she was saddened by the miserable living conditions she found around her. By 1917 she was working for a socialist paper and took part in a hunger strike. She later joined the women's suffrage movement and was jailed for her involvement. Through these experiences, Dorothy gained a greater sense of the presence of God and was less concerned by her own poverty. In 1932 she started the newspaper *Catholic Worker* out of a vision she had for a social reform movement within Catholicism. She also opened up a soup kitchen and hospitality houses around New York City. In the 1940s she wrote her autobiography, *The Long Loneliness*. Throughout her life, Dorothy modeled what it means to live in communion with God as well as in small communities, stressing the sacredness of every person. She was often jailed for her opposition to humanitarian issues, such as war and poor wages for farm workers. She lived out the Christian calling to have mercy on the poor and was an active pacifist.

What is the Relationship between the History of Women's Leadership in the Church and Where We Are Today?

Our investigation of church history has revealed that there has never been such a thing as constant progress or forward movement on the issue of women's full equality and participation in all areas of ministry. For all of the times when women have been recognized and allowed to serve in positions of authority there have been just as many, if not more, times of suppression and silencing. In relationship to the status of women in ministry in the church today, the view we gain from a historical perspective allows us to realize that for every corner of equality and opportunity today, there are just as many, if not more, areas where women need more support and where full equality is not being lived out. Just as our picture of history does not allow either a completely negative assessment of women's place in the church nor a wholly celebratory one, neither does our current situation today allow us to rest on our laurels or to throw up our hands in defeat. Gains made by women in the church are indeed real and significant. On the other hand, biblical literalism and traditional views of women's roles have made it very nearly impossible for many churches to even consider the idea of a woman pastor.[8]

What we can say most definitely is that the voices and stories of women from the church's past are absolutely critical in providing valuable insights needed for creating change and recovering the prophetic voice of gifted, Spirit-filled women within the church. Moreover, our hope is that women today would be encouraged by the perseverance of those women leaders who have gone before them, women who were never permanently silenced or erased, women who, with every attempt at marginalization, remained re-markably resilient and able to almost mysteriously materialize in another corner of the church. What the church has needed and always will need is the strong witness and leading presence of Spirit-filled women to share the good news and enact it into the daily life of the church community and the world that so desperately needs its transforming power.

For Reflection

1. What is your overall impression regarding the role of women in ministry throughout church history?

2. What remaining questions do you have?

Testimony: The Reverend Julie Hoplamazian

The Reverend Julie Hoplamazian holds a BS in Music Education from Gettysburg College and an MDiv from Princeton Theological Seminary. Before joining the Episcopal Church, Julie served in the Armenian Orthodox Church as the Coordinator of College Ministry.

8. MacHaffie, *Her Story*, 153.

In 2012 Julie was called as the Assistant Rector at Grace Church Brooklyn Heights, where she currently serves. Julie and her husband, Jeremy, are animal lovers and enjoy the company of their sidekick Takouhi ("queen" in Armenian), a rescued Australian Shepherd mutt.

It is hard to pin down an exact time or place that initiated my call to ordained ministry. I can identify memories and experiences throughout my childhood when echoes of that call began, and there were seasons of life, such as college, summer camp, and high school youth group when the contours of my calling began to take shape. I still remember the moment, as if it was yesterday, when, in a college New Testament course, I discovered that women could be ordained as pastors, and I suddenly realized that a whole new world had been opened up to me.

Memories and moments aside, there is no denying that the journey from my Armenian Catholic and Armenian Orthodox upbringing, where the only role for "ordained" women was that of a nun, to my current position as an ordained Episcopal priest, has been anything but linear. Yet I always knew, deep down, that I was called to ordained ministry long before I ever took my first steps down that path. Leaving behind not only a religious tradition but also a cultural community, which, in the Armenian Church, are extremely intertwined, was not something I was excited to do. I love my Armenian heritage, and I find the ancient traditions of the Catholic and Orthodox churches beautiful and transcendent in many ways. But more than that, I love God, and my soul's deepest thirst was to consecrate my life to God. In the Catholic and Orthodox churches that means ordination, to be "set aside for a holy purpose."

Through my seminary studies and my work as a lay minister in the Armenian Orthodox Church, both as a youth minister in a parish, and as a campus ministry coordinator at the national level, I came to realize that I was literally being set aside for the "holy" purpose of a church tradition that revered patriarchy and the safety of ancient language more than the movement of the holy Spirit in our lives. In my experience, it was all too common to hear priests and bishops passing the buck back to God, saying that their hands were tied by tradition, reciting how the church has done it this way for two thousand years, and reasoning that if God gave us this tradition, then who are we to say that God is wrong. On this topic, I learned, you are not allowed to question God. But that is exactly what I did. I wondered where God was, living and moving and breathing, in our church today. I wondered why there was so much fear and protection of power among our clergy, and why honest and open dialogue about the ordination of women was not permitted. I wondered why censorship and silencing dissent were the only ways the Armenian Church dealt with this issue. I wondered why there had not been an Armenian saint canonized in over five hundred years, and how the church expected its people to feel empowered to be followers of Christ when it was not able to produce any notable ones in over five centuries.

I came to view the Armenian Church as a museum piece, something ancient and fragile that had to be protected. Its customs, language, and traditions had been threatened almost to the point of utter annihilation during the Armenian Genocide of 1915, but, nearly a century later, its people were still in survival mode. I realized that the church was not interested in the breath and fresh movement of the holy Spirit, because that would mean opening the doors to the possibility of change, and the church was too fearful of change to allow for the growth that might come with it. Despite the fact that the ordination of women might actually help the church to grow, patriarchy (and misogyny, if I am honest) had become too woven into the fabric of church tradition.

And so my journey has been about learning how to be Armenian on my own terms, rather than on the terms the community defined, and figuring out how to incorporate elements of my ancient church tradition into my ministry in the Episcopal Church, where I have found not only a home but also more openness to the power of the holy Spirit in our lives. I feel so blessed to be part of a church that continues to ask how God compels us to live out the gospel in our own communities as well as on a larger scale in twenty-first-century America. I love being a priest. I cannot imagine doing anything else with my life's calling. And now, I finally do feel set aside for a holy purpose: leading others in the truth of the gospel as we seek to be God's light in the world.

For Reflection

1. Reflect for a moment on Julie's estimation that the Armenian Orthodox church revered patriarchy and the safety of ancient language more than the movement of the holy Spirit in our lives. What does she mean? What do you think about this?

2. How would you respond to a priest or bishop who argued that two thousand years of church tradition should not be overturned in order to allow women to be ordained to ministry?

What Remains to be Done?

The ability and freedom of qualified Christian men to participate fully in the ministry and leadership of Christ's church is already affirmed *de facto*. Yet for qualified Christian women to do the same is often still a topic of hot debate and for many the jury is still out. Throughout this study we have sought to consider the question "Does Scripture exclude women from full participation in all forms of ministry simply on the basis of gender?" We have looked at theology, the rule of faith, Scripture, church history, and a myriad of experiences of Christian women past and present to shed light on this often complex and even confusing topic. At the outset of this study, I admitted that in my estimation it seems clear that God calls certain women to lead and serve as pastors and ordained ministers in the church just as God calls certain men to do the same.

And so we might wonder, are qualified Christian women indeed leading and ministering to church congregations on either the local or denominational level? In many cases, they are. However, many churches and denominations will not consider the possibility. Other churches and denominations have written statements expressing their affirmation of the appropriateness of women's full participation but have yet to enact such "beliefs" either partially or completely.

As the church continues to pray for the reign of God to come to full fruition and for God's will to be done on earth as it is in heaven, so we also need to strive for women's full participation in the ministry and mission of the church. For some this will mean accepting God's call on their lives and courageously pursuing it despite the opposition they may face. For others it will mean learning to support and encourage qualified Christian women to use their God-given gifts for the enhancement of the body of Christ. Many churches will need to adopt a pro-active stance of seeking women's leadership in roles they have yet to assume. This will mean not only asking women to fill these roles but also encouraging girls and young women to pray about how God might be calling them and reminding them that all positions are open. Denominations will need to open up networking possibilities to include women and continually have on their agenda the topic of women's full inclusion in the leadership of the church denomination.

The road ahead of us might be long and hard, but at the end of the day we are not left to our own devices. The work is God's, and we are partners with Christ through the holy Spirit. Our hope was given to us in the resurrection of Christ from the dead, and we look forward to the day when Christ returns and God's reign will be established completely. Christian women and men will be perfectly complete, as the triune God is perfect. All forms of injustice will be abolished and reconciliation between all people, churches, nations, systems, and structures will occur. Until then we continue to tarry and strive under the power of the holy Spirit. Let us pray together, "Come, Lord Jesus. Have your way in us and use us as you will. Do not let us get in the way of the work you have called your church to do."

For Reflection

1. What is God saying to you about your responsibility in what remains to be done?

2. Consider your thoughts about women in ministry as you stated them at the beginning of this study. Have your thoughts and beliefs changed at all? Why or why not?

Bibliography

Bassler, Jouette M. *1 Timothy, 2 Timothy, Titus*. Abingdon New Testament Commentaries. Nashville: Abingdon, 1996.

Bristow, John Temple. *What Paul Really Said about Women: An Apostle's Liberating Views on Equality in Marriage, Leadership, and Love*. New York: HarperCollins, 1988.

Congdon, David W. "Trinity, Gender, and Subordination: A Response to the Trinitarian Argument for Complementarianism." Pages 1–26. Online: http://www.academia.edu/7863514/Trinity_Gender_and_Subordination _A_Response_to_the_Trinitarian_Argument_for_Complementarianism.

Fee, Gordon D. *The First Epistle to the Corinthians*. New International Commentary on the New Testament Series. Grand Rapids: Eerdmans, 1987.

———. "The Priority of Spirit Gifting for Church Ministry." In *Discovering Biblical Equality: Complementarity Without Hierarchy*, edited by Ronald W. Pierce and Rebecca Merrill Groothuis, 241–54. Downers Grove, IL: InterVarsity Academic, 2005.

Giles, Kevin. "A Critique of the 'Novel' Contemporary Interpretation of 1 Timothy 2:9–15 Given in the Book *Women in the Church*. Part II." *Evangelical Quarterly* 72 (2000) 195–215.

Gregory of Nyssa. *Commentary on the Song of Songs*. Translated by Casimir McCambley. Brookline, MA: Hellenic College Press, 1987.

Johnson, Luke Timothy. *The First and Second Letters to Timothy*. The Anchor Yale Bible Commentaries. New Haven, CT: Yale University Press, 2001.

Kroeger, Richard Clark, and Catherine Clark Kroeger. *I Suffer Not a Woman: Rethinking 1 Timothy 2:11–15 in Light of Ancient Evidence*. Grand Rapids: Baker, 1992.

LaCelle-Peterson, Kristina. *Liberating Tradition: Women's Identity and Vocation in Christian Perspective*. Grand Rapids: Baker Academic, 2008.

Levison, Jack. "Thrill Ride: Acts 1–2." In *Lectio: Guided Bible Reading (blog)*, *The Center for Biblical and Theological Education*. Acts Week 2. Seattle Pacific University. Online: http://blog.spu.edu/lectio/thrill-ride/.

MacHaffie, Barbara J. *Her Story: Women in Christian Tradition*. Philadelphia: Fortress, 1986.

Malone, Mary T. *Women and Christianity: Volume I: The First Thousand Years*. Ontario: Novalis, 2000.

Marshall, Celia Brewer. *A Guide through the Old Testament*. Louisville: Westminster John Knox, 1989.

Marshall, Sherrin, ed. *Women in Reformation and Counter-Reformation Europe: Private and Public Worlds*. Bloomington, IN: Indiana University Press, 1989.

McKnight, Scot. *The Blue Parakeet: Rethinking How You Read the Bible*. Grand Rapids: Zondervan, 2008.

Oden, Thomas C. *First and Second Timothy and Titus*. Interpretation: A Bible Commentary for Teaching and Preaching. Grand Rapids: Westminster John Knox, 1989.

Padgett, Alan G. *As Christ Submits to the Church: A Biblical Understanding of Leadership and Mutual Submission*. Grand Rapids: Baker Academic, 2011.

Pope-Levison, Priscilla. *Turn the Pulpit Loose: Two Centuries of American Women Evangelists*. New York: Palgrave, 2004.

Radner, Ephraim. *A Brutal Unity: The Spiritual Politics of the Christian Church*. Waco, TX: Baylor University Press, 2012.

———. *The End of the Church: A Pneumatology of Christian Division in the West*. Grand Rapids: Eerdmans, 1998.

Sakenfeld, Katharine Doob. *Just Wives? Stories of Power and Survival in the Old Testament and Today*. Louisville: Westminster John Knox, 2003.

Schneiders, Sandra M. *Written that You May Believe: Encountering Jesus in the Fourth Gospel*. New York: Crossroad, 1999.

Smythe, Shannon. "Gender Reconciliation, All the Way Down: 1 Corinthians 11:2–16; Galatians 3:26–28; Genesis 1:26–28." In *Lectio: Guided Bible Reading (blog), The Center for Biblical and Theological Education*. Selections on New Creation Week 8. Seattle Pacific University. http://blog. spu.edu/lectio/gender-reconciliation-all-the-way-down/.

Spencer, Aída Besançon. *Beyond the Curse: Women Called to Ministry*. Nashville: Thomas Nelson, 1985.

Tanner, Kathryn. *Christ the Key*. Cambridge: Cambridge University Press, 2010.

Torjesen, Karen Jo. *When Women Were Priests: Women's Leadership in the Early Church and the Scandal of their Subordination in the Rise of Christianity*. San Francisco: HarperSanFrancisco, 1993.

Wall, Robert W. *1 & 2 Timothy and Titus*. With Richard B. Steele. The Two Horizons New Testament Commentary. Grand Rapids: Eerdmans, 2012.

———. "1 Timothy 2:9–15 Reconsidered (Again)." *Bulletin for Biblical Research* 14.1 (2004) 81–103.

———. "Canonical Context and Canonical Conversations." In *Between Two Horizons: Spanning New Testament Studies and Systematic Theology*, edited by Joel B. Green and Max Turner, 165–82. Grand Rapids: Eerdmans, 2000.

———. "Reading the Bible from within Our Traditions: The 'Rule of Faith' in Theological Hermeneutics." In *Between Two Horizons: Spanning New*

Testament Studies and Systematic Theology, edited by Joel B. Green and Max Turner, 88–107. Grand Rapids: Eerdmans, 2000.

Wilke, D. "Gospel Light Worldwide Continues the Legacy of Dr. Henrietta Mears." In *Our Heritage Gospel Light Worldwide*. No pages. Online: http://gospellightworldwide.org/2012/11/07/gospel-light-worldwide -continues-the-legacy-of-dr-henrietta-mears/.

Williams, Don. *The Apostle Paul and Women in the Church*. Van Nuys, CA: BIM, 1977.

Made in the USA
Monee, IL
08 September 2019